Hanukkah in L....

M000073317

Bring the Past to Light

with Moshe Pearlman's readings for families

History • Songs • Celebration

Marian Scheuer Sofaer

Book design and layout by SingerSiddur
www.singersiddur.com

Cover illustrations and drawings of oil lamp and ancient pot
by Dr. Joan Scheuer

Drawings of scroll with music and Greek soldier
by Marianne Aaron

Photos and drawings of ancient coins
from a private collection on loan to the American Numismatic Society
Used by permission of the owners

Selected Hebrew texts and fonts
Copyright © Davka Corporation
Used by permission

1. Hanukkah – Young Adult.   2. Jews – History – Maccabean period
3. Holidays – Jewish – Chanukah

ISBN 0-9774768-0-4
ISBN13 9780977476800

Hanukkah in Eight Nights: Bring the Past to Light
with Moshe Pearlman's readings for families
Copyright ©2005 Marian Scheuer Sofaer
All rights reserved.

mss114@columbia.edu

In memory of Moshe Pearlman

and his sister, Pearl Ketcher, M.D.

ז"ל

Author's Note

Hanukkah is a holiday based on real events in Jewish history. We celebrate it to brighten up the winter months, and also to teach our children about the Jewish people's struggle for independence in the second century B.C.E. This focus on the history of the Maccabean period is a link between our past and our present. When we integrate the history of the Maccabees and their world into our Hanukkah celebrations, we learn about their struggle to maintain Jewish intellectual and religious traditions. This is still an issue in the complex world in which we live today.

Acknowledgments

Moshe Pearlman wrote eight readings for Hanukkah in 1980, adapting them from his 1973 book, *The Maccabees*, published by Macmillan Publishing Co., NY in 1973, and Weidenfeld & Nicolson, London. Moshe's brother, David Pearlman, and the Pearlman family kindly gave permission to publish the readings.

Roslyn Schloss, expert editor and friend, provided invaluable assistance. Alain Rossman and Joanna Hoffman's historical summary, Dan Sofaer's translation from the Greek, David Hendin's description of Maccabean coins, and Ilana Panker's help with recipes make it a more comprehensive source for home celebrations. Dr. Trude Dothan, Dr. Sy Gittin and Dr. Adrian Leveen reviewed sections of the book, and Vivian Singer of SingerSiddur made it all work. Dr. Joan G. Scheuer did the cover illustrations.

This book wouldn't have found its way to print without Richard Jonas Scheuer, who asked Moshe Pearlman for a manuscript for a home Hanukkah celebration many years ago, and who always has the big picture. I thank my husband Abe, and my children, who share an interest in Jewish history.

– Marian Scheuer Sofaer

Table of Contents

THE HANUKKAH BLESSINGS 1

Hanerot Halalu 2

SONGS 3

Maoz Tzur 3

Dreidel 5

S'vivon 6

Mi Y'maleil 7

Banu Chosech 8

Hanukkah 9

Hanukkah, O Hanukkah 10

Ner Li 12

Ocho Kandelikas 13

Hatikvah 14

DRAMATIC READINGS BY MOSHE PEARLMAN

WITH EXCERPTS FROM THE ANCIENT SOURCES
TRANSLATED FROM GREEK
BY DAN SOFAER 15

First Light: The Desecration 15

Quotations from Josephus,
I and II Maccabees, Athenaeus 17

Second Light: The Martyrs 18

Quotations from II and IV Maccabees 20

Third Light: The Revolt 23

Quotations from I Maccabees 25

Fourth Light: The Resistance Fighters 26

Quotations from I Maccabees 28

Fifth Light: Judah the Maccabee 29

Quotation from I Maccabees 31

Sixth Light: The Test 32

Quotation from I Maccabees 35

Seventh Light: The Battles 36

Quotations from I Maccabees 38

Eighth Light: The Temple Regained 39

Quotations from I Maccabees 41

HANUKKAH CHRONOLOGY
AND QUESTIONS FOR DISCUSSION 42
Hanukkah Chronology 42
Questions for Discussion 45

STORIES FROM 1 MACCABEES 46
Notes on the ancient sources 59

TRADITIONAL HANUKKAH RECIPES 60
Latkes (Potato Pancakes) 60
Sufganiyot (Jelly Doughnuts) 61
Hlawa – An Iraqi Hanukkah Treat 62

A VERY BRIEF JEWISH HISTORY
FROM THE PATRIARCHAL PERIOD TO THE MACCABEES
BY ALAIN ROSSMANN AND JOANNA HOFFMAN
.... 64

COINS OF THE MACCABEES
BY DAVID HENDIN 72

DREIDEL GAME 74

PLAN AHEAD FOR HOME HANUKKAH CELEBRATIONS
.... 76

Bronze prutah of Mattathias Antigonus (40-37 B.C.E.)

Obverse:
The shew-bread table of the Temple with Hebrew inscription:
MATTITYAHU
Reverse:
The Temple Menorah with Greek inscription:
BASILEOS ANT[IGONUS]

The Hanukkah Blessings

בָּרוּךְ אַתָּה יְיָ אֱלֹהֵינוּ מֶלֶךְ הָעוֹלָם,
אֲשֶׁר קִדְּשָׁנוּ בְּמִצְוֹתָיו, וְצִוָּנוּ לְהַדְלִיק נֵר שֶׁל חֲנֻכָּה.

Baruch ata Adonai Eloheinu melech ha-olam,
asher kidshanu b'mitsvotav, v'tzivanu l'hadlik ner shel chanuka.

Blessed art thou, Lord our God, King of the Universe,
who has sanctified us with His commandments and commanded us
to light the Hanukkah candles.

בָּרוּךְ אַתָּה יְיָ אֱלֹהֵינוּ מֶלֶךְ הָעוֹלָם,
שֶׁעָשָׂה נִסִּים לַאֲבוֹתֵינוּ בַּיָּמִים הָהֵם בַּזְּמַן הַזֶּה.

Baruch ata Adonai Eloheinu melech ha-olam,
she-asa nisim la-avoteinu bayamim hahem bazman hazeh.

Blessed art thou, Lord our God, King of the Universe, who made
miracles for our forefathers, in those days, in this season.

On the first night, add:

בָּרוּךְ אַתָּה יְיָ אֱלֹהֵינוּ מֶלֶךְ הָעוֹלָם,
שֶׁהֶחֱיָנוּ וְקִיְּמָנוּ וְהִגִּיעָנוּ לַזְּמַן הַזֶּה.

Baruch ata Adonai, Eloheinu melech ha-olam,
sheheche-yanu v'ki-y'manu v'higi-yanu lazman hazeh.

Blessed art thou, Lord our God, King of the Universe,
who granted us life, and sustained us, and brought us to this day.

Hanerot Halalu

After lighting the candles:

הַנֵּרוֹת הַלָּלוּ אֲנַחְנוּ מַדְלִיקִים עַל הַנִּסִּים וְעַל הַנִּפְלָאוֹת וְעַל
הַתְּשׁוּעוֹת וְעַל הַמִּלְחָמוֹת שֶׁעָשִׂיתָ לַאֲבוֹתֵינוּ בַּיָּמִים הָהֶם
בַּזְּמַן הַזֶּה, עַל יְדֵי כֹּהֲנֶיךָ הַקְּדוֹשִׁים. וְכָל שְׁמוֹנַת יְמֵי חֲנֻכָּה
הַנֵּרוֹת הַלָּלוּ קֹדֶשׁ הֵם, וְאֵין לָנוּ רְשׁוּת לְהִשְׁתַּמֵּשׁ בָּהֶם, אֶלָּא
לִרְאוֹתָם בִּלְבָד, כְּדֵי לְהוֹדוֹת וּלְהַלֵּל לְשִׁמְךָ הַגָּדוֹל, עַל נִסֶּיךָ
וְעַל נִפְלְאוֹתֶיךָ וְעַל יְשׁוּעָתֶךָ.

Haneirot halalu anu madlikim, al hanisim, v'al hanifla-ot, v'al hat'shu-ot, v'al hamil-chamot she-asita la-avoteinu bayamim hahem bazman hazeh, al y'dei cohanecha hak'doshim. V'chol sh'monat y'mei chanuka, haneirot halalu kodesh heim, v'ein lanu r'shut l'hishtameish bahem, eleh lirotam bilvad, k'dei l'hodot ul'haleil l'shimcha hagadol, al nisecha v'al nifl'otecha v'al y'shu-atecha.

These lights that we kindle: they commemorate saving our forefathers with miracles and wonders, in those days, at this season, through Your holy priests. All eight days of Hanukkah, these candles will be sacred, and we will gaze at them but not use them, in order to give thanks and praise Your great name, and Your miracles, wonders, and saving acts.

Note: This is an ancient song that is mentioned in the Talmud.

Songs

Maoz Tzur

Ma'oz Tzur is sung after lighting the Hanukkiah. Scholars believe it was written in Germany in the 13th century by a poet named Mordechai, whose name appears in an acrostic. The standard melody is Ashkenazi and is said to date from the beginning of the 15th century.

Ma-oz tzur y'shu-ati

l'cha na-eh l'shabei-ach,

tikon beit t'filati

v'sham toda n'zabei-ach,

l'eit tachin matbei-ach

mitzar ham-nabei-ach,

az egmor

b'shir mizmor

chanukat hamizbei-ach.

מָעוֹז צוּר יְשׁוּעָתִי

לְךָ נָאֶה לְשַׁבֵּחַ,

תִּכּוֹן בֵּית תְּפִלָּתִי

וְשָׁם תּוֹדָה נְזַבֵּחַ,

לְעֵת תָּכִין מַטְבֵּחַ

מִצָּר הַמְנַבֵּחַ,

אָז אֶגְמוֹר

בְּשִׁיר מִזְמוֹר

חֲנֻכַּת הַמִּזְבֵּחַ.

Rock of Ages let our song
Praise Thy saving power;
Thou amidst the raging foes;
Wast our sheltering tower.

Furious they assailed us,
But Thine arm availed us,
And Thy word broke their sword,
When our own strength failed us.

Children of the Maccabees
Whether free or fettered,
Wake the echoes of the songs
Where ye may be scattered.

Yours the message cheering
That the time is nearing
Which will see all men free
And tyrants disappearing.

– Rabbi Gustav Gottheil
(1827–1903)

Additional verses of Maoz Tzur:

רָעוֹת שָׂבְעָה נַפְשִׁי   בְּיָגוֹן כֹּחִי כָּלָה,
חַיַּי מֵרְרוּ בְקֹשִׁי   בְּשִׁעְבּוּד מַלְכוּת עֶגְלָה,
וּבְיָדוֹ הַגְּדוֹלָה   הוֹצִיא אֶת הַסְּגֻלָּה,
חֵיל פַּרְעֹה וְכָל זַרְעוֹ   יָרְדוּ כְאֶבֶן מְצוּלָה.

דְּבִיר קָדְשׁוֹ הֱבִיאַנִי   וְגַם שָׁם לֹא שָׁקַטְתִּי,
וּבָא נוֹגֵשׂ וְהִגְלַנִי   כִּי זָרִים עָבַדְתִּי,
וְיֵין רַעַל מָסַכְתִּי   כִּמְעַט שֶׁעָבַרְתִּי,
קֵץ בָּבֶל, זְרֻבָּבֶל,   לְקֵץ שִׁבְעִים נוֹשַׁעְתִּי.

כְּרֹת קוֹמַת בְּרוֹשׁ בִּקֵּשׁ   אֲגָגִי בֶּן הַמְּדָתָא,
וְנִהְיְתָה לוֹ לְפַח וּלְמוֹקֵשׁ   וְגַאֲוָתוֹ נִשְׁבָּתָה,
רֹאשׁ יְמִינִי נִשֵּׂאתָ,   וְאוֹיֵב שְׁמוֹ מָחִיתָ,
רֹב בָּנָיו וְקִנְיָנָיו   עַל הָעֵץ תָּלִיתָ.

יְוָנִים נִקְבְּצוּ עָלַי   אֲזַי בִּימֵי חַשְׁמַנִּים,
וּפָרְצוּ חוֹמוֹת מִגְדָּלַי   וְטִמְּאוּ כָּל הַשְּׁמָנִים,
וּמִנּוֹתַר קַנְקַנִּים   נַעֲשָׂה נֵס לַשּׁוֹשַׁנִּים,
בְּנֵי בִינָה יְמֵי שְׁמוֹנָה   קָבְעוּ שִׁיר וּרְנָנִים.

חֲשׂוֹף זְרוֹעַ קָדְשֶׁךָ   וְקָרֵב קֵץ הַיְשׁוּעָה,
נְקֹם נִקְמַת דַּם עֲבָדֶיךָ   מֵאֻמָּה הָרְשָׁעָה,
כִּי אָרְכָה לָנוּ הַיְשׁוּעָה,   וְאֵין קֵץ לִימֵי הָרָעָה,
דְּחֵה אַדְמוֹן בְּצֵל צַלְמוֹן   הָקֵם לָנוּ רוֹעִים שִׁבְעָה

Dreidel

I have a little dreidel,
I made it out of clay.
And when it's dry and ready,
Then dreidel I shall play!

Chorus:
Oh dreidel, dreidel, dreidel,
I made it out of clay.
Oh dreidel, dreidel, dreidel,
Now dreidel I shall play!

It has a lovely body,
With leg so short and thin.
And when it is all tired,
It drops and then I win!

Oh dreidel, dreidel, dreidel,
With leg so short and thin.
Oh dreidel, dreidel, dreidel,
It drops and then I win!

My dreidel's always playful,.
It loves to dance and spin.
A happy game of dreidel,
Come play now, let's begin!

Oh dreidel, dreidel, dreidel,
It loves to dance and spin.
Oh dreidel, dreidel, dreidel,
Come play now, let's begin!

– Lyrics: Samuel Grossman
Music: Samuel Eliezer Goldfarb

Samuel Goldfarb, who was born in Russia in 1897, wrote the music for this popular song. He was the music director at the Bureau of Jewish Education in New York City from 1910 to 1929, and he played the Wurlitzer organ in movie theaters for silent movies.

S'vivon

S'vivon, sov, sov, sov	סְבִיבוֹן, סֹב, סֹב, סֹב!
Chanuka, hu chag tov	חֲנֻכָּה הוּא חַג טוֹב,
Chanuka, hu chag tov	חֲנֻכָּה הוּא חַג טוֹב,
S'vivon, sov, sov, sov!	סְבִיבוֹן, סֹב, סֹב, סֹב!
Sov na sov, ko vacho,	סֹב נָא סֹב, כֹּה וָכֹה,
Nes gadol haya po.	נֵס גָּדוֹל הָיָה פֹּה!
Chag simcha hu la-am	חַג שִׂמְחָה הוּא לָעָם,
Nes gadol haya sham	נֵס גָּדוֹל הָיָה שָׁם,
Nes gadol haya sham	נֵס גָּדוֹל הָיָה שָׁם,
Chag simcha hu la-am.	חַג שִׂמְחָה הוּא לָעָם.

– Lyrics: Levin Kipnis (the Ukraine, 1894–Tel Aviv, 1990)

An English version:

S'vivon, turn and turn,
While the lovely candles burn,
What a wondrous holiday,
Watch us sing and dance and play.
Tell the story full of cheer,
A great miracle happened there.
It's a festival of light
for eight days and eight nights.

– S. Gewirtz

Mi Y'maleil

Mi y'maleil g'vurot Yisra-eil?	מִי יְמַלֵּל גְּבוּרוֹת יִשְׂרָאֵל?
Otan mi yimneh?	אוֹתָן מִי יִמְנֶה?
Hein b'chol dor yakum hagibor	הֵן בְּכָל דּוֹר יָקוּם הַגִּבּוֹר
go-eil ha-am.	גּוֹאֵל הָעָם.
Sh'ma!	שְׁמַע!
Bayamim ha-heim bazman hazeh	בַּיָּמִים הָהֵם בַּזְּמַן הַזֶּה
Makabi moshi-a ufodeh	מַכַּבִּי מוֹשִׁיעַ וּפוֹדֶה.
Uv-yameinu kol am Yisra-eil,	וּבְיָמֵינוּ כָּל עַם יִשְׂרָאֵל
yit-acheid yakum l'higa-eil.	יִתְאַחֵד יָקוּם לְהִגָּאֵל!

An English version to sing:

Who can retell the things that befell us?
Who can count them?
In every age a hero or sage
Came to our aid.

Hark! In days of yore in Israel's ancient land,
Brave Maccabeus led the faithful band.
But now all Israel must as one arise,
Redeem itself through deed and sacrifice.

Who can retell the things that befell us?
Who can count them?
In every age a hero or sage
Came to our aid.

– Samuel Rosenbaum
and B. M. Edidin

Banu Choshech

Banu choshech l'garesh,	בָּאנוּ חֹשֶׁךְ לְגָרֵשׁ.
b'yadeinu or va-esh.	בְּיָדֵנוּ אוֹר וָאֵשׁ
Kol echad hu or katan,	כָּל אֶחָד הוּא אוֹר קָטָן,
v'chulanu or eitan.	וְכֻלָּנוּ – אוֹר אֵיתָן.
Sura choshech, hal'a sh'chor!	סוּרָה חֹשֶׁךְ, הָלְאָה שְׁחוֹר!
Sura mipnei ha-or!	סוּרָה – מִפְּנֵי הָאוֹר!

– Lyrics: Sarah Levi Tanai

Literal translation:

> We came to banish darkness
> With light and fire in our hands
> Each one of us is a small light
> And together – a strong light
>
> Darkness, away! Blackness, be off!
> Scram, away from the light!

An English version to sing:

> As we march, the dark we fight;
> In our hands, there's fire and light.
> Each of us is one small light;
> Now, as one, the light is bright.
>
> Vanish, darkness, out of sight;
> Scram, now, we bring the light.

Hanukkah

Chanuka, Chanuka,	חֲנֻכָּה, חֲנֻכָּה,
chag yafeh kol-cach!	חַג יָפֶה כָּל-כָּךְ!
Chag shel or, chag shel dror,	חַג שֶׁל אוֹר, חַג שֶׁל דְּרוֹר,
mi zeh lo yismach?	מִי זֶה לֹא יִשְׂמַח?
Al kol kir, ner maz-hir,	עַל כָּל קִיר, נֵר מַזְהִיר,
al migdal vagag –	עַל מִגְדָּל וָגָג –
shiru na: Chanuka,	שִׁירוּ נָא: חֲנֻכָּה,
ein kamohu chag!	אֵין כָּמוֹהוּ חַג!
Chanuka, Chanuka,	חֲנֻכָּה, חֲנֻכָּה,
chag chaviv marnin!	חַג חָבִיב מַרְנִין!
L'vivot m'tukot	לְבִיבוֹת מְתוּקוֹת,
kol ima tachin.	כָּל אִמָּא תָּכִין.
Lapidim, rikudim,	לַפִּידִים, רִקוּדִים,
s'vivon sov-sov,	סְבִיבוֹן, סֹב-סֹב!
sov-sov-sov, sov-sov-sov –	סֹב-סֹב-סֹב, סֹב-סֹב-סֹב –
Chanuka chag tov!	חֲנֻכָּה חַג טוֹב!

– Levin Kipnis (the Ukraine, 1894–Tel Aviv, 1990)

Translation:

Hanukkah, Hanukkah, such a beautiful festival!
A festival of light, a festival of freedom,
who wouldn't be happy?
On every wall, a candle shines, on tower and on wall.
Sing, then, Hanukkah, there's no festival like it!

Hanukkah, Hanukkah, beloved festival, we sing with joy
Sweet latkes every mother makes,
Torches, dances, dreidel, turn, turn,
Turn, turn, turn, turn, turn, turn.
Hanukkah is a good festival!

Hanukkah, O Hanukkah

יְמֵי הַחֲנֻכָּה חֲנֻכַּת מִקְדָּשֵׁנוּ
בְּגִיל וּבְשִׂמְחָה מְמַלְאִים אֶת לִבֵּנוּ
לַיְלָה וָיוֹם סְבִיבוֹנֵנוּ יִסֹּב
סֻפְגָּנִיּוֹת נֹאכַל בָּם לָרֹב
הָאִירוּ הַדְלִיקוּ נֵרוֹת חֲנֻכָּה רַבִּים
עַל הַנִּסִּים וְעַל הַנִּפְלָאוֹת אֲשֶׁר חוֹלְלוּ הַמַּכַּבִּים

Hanukkah, O Hanukkah, come light the Menorah
Let's have a party, we'll all dance the hora
Gather round the table, we'll all have a treat
S'vivon to play with, and latkes to eat.

And while we are playing
The candles are burning low
One for each night, they shed a sweet light
To remind us of days long ago.

One for each night, they shed a sweet light
To remind us of days long ago.

Two versions in Yiddish:

Chanukkah, O Chanukkah
A yontev a sheyner
A lustiger a freylicher
Nito noch azoyner
Ale nacht in dreydl shpiln mir
Zudigheyse latkes esn mir
Geshvinder tsindt kinder
Di dininke lichtelech on
Zogt "al ha-nisim," loybt G-t far di nisim
Un kumt gicher tantsn in kon

Oy Chanukah oy Chanukah, a yontif a sheiner
A lustiker a freylicher nito noch a zeyner
Alle nacht in dreydlech shpiln mir
Zudik hesse latkes essen mir
Geshvinder tsindt kinder
di Chanukah lichtelech on
Zol yeder bazunder bazingen dem vunder
un tantzen freylech in kohn (2x)

Ner Li

Ner li, ner li	נֵר לִי, נֵר לִי,
ner li dakik.	נֵר לִי דָקִיק.
Bachanuka	בַּחֲנֻכָּה
neri ya-ir.	נֵרִי יָאִיר.
Bachanuka	בַּחֲנֻכָּה
shirim ashir.	שִׁירִים אָשִׁיר.
La, la	לָ, לְ ...

– D. Sambursky & L. Kipnis

I have a candle, a candle so light
On Chanukah my candle burns bright.

On Chanukah its light burns long
On Chanukah I sing this song.
La, la ...

Ocho Kandelikas
(Ladino)

Chanukah linda sta aki, ocho kandelas para mi
Chanukah linda sta aki, ocho kandelas para mi

> *O – Una kandelika, dos kandelikas,*
> *tres kandelikas, kuatro kandelikas,*
> *sintyu kandelikas, sej kandelikas,*
> *siete kandelikas, ocho kandelas para mi*

Muchas fiestas vo fazer, kon alegriyas y plazer
Muchas fiestas vo fazer, kon alegriyas y plazer

> *O – Una kandelika, dos kandelikas,*
> *tres kandelikas, kuatro kandelikas,*
> *sintyu kandelikas, sej kandelikas,*
> *siete kandelikas, ocho kandelas para mi*

Los pastelikos vo kumer, kon almendrikas y la myel
Los pastelikos vo kumer, kon almendrikas y la myel

> *O – Una kandelika, dos kandelikas,*
> *tres kandelikas, kuatro kandelikas,*
> *sintyu kandelikas, sej kandelikas,*
> *siete kandelikas, ocho kandelas para mi*

– Flory Jagoda

Translation:

Beautiful Chanukah is here, eight candles for me.
One candle, two candles, three candles, four candles,
five candles, six candles, seven candles, eight candles for me.

Many parties will be held, with joy and with pleasure.
One candle...

I will cook pastelikas (a Sephardic delicacy)
with almonds and honey.
One candle...

Hatikvah

Kol od baleivav p'nima	כָּל עוֹד בַּלֵּבָב פְּנִימָה
nefesh y'hudi homi-ya	נֶפֶשׁ יְהוּדִי הוֹמִיָּה
ul'fa-atei mizrach kadima	וּלְפַאֲתֵי מִזְרָח קָדִימָה
ayin l'tzi-yon tzofi-yah.	עַיִן לְצִיּוֹן צוֹפִיָּה.
Od lo avda tikvateinu	עוֹד לֹא אָבְדָה תִּקְוָתֵנוּ
hatikvah sh'not alpayim	הַתִּקְוָה שְׁנוֹת אַלְפַּיִם
li-h'yot am chof-shi b'artzeinu	לִהְיוֹת עַם חָפְשִׁי בְּאַרְצֵנוּ
eretz tzi-yon virushala-yim.	אֶרֶץ צִיּוֹן וִירוּשָׁלַיִם.

As long as the Jewish spirit is yearning deep in the heart,
With eyes turned toward the East, looking toward Zion,
Then our hope – the two-thousand-year-old hope – will not be lost:
To be a free people in our land, the land of Zion and Jerusalem.

– Naphtali Herz Imber, 1886

Dramatic Readings by Moshe Pearlman with excerpts from the ancient sources translated from Greek by Dan Sofaer

First Light: The Desecration

In the Jewish village on Modi'in, seventeen miles north of Jerusalem, a priest named Mattathias sat in silence on the floor of his home together with his five sons, Johanan, Simon, Judah, Eleazar, and Jonathan. Like all their fellow Jews in Judea, they had gone into deep mourning upon learning that the sacred Temple in Jerusalem had been desecrated. Now they sat, heads bowed, eyes downcast, fists clenched, grimly wondering what could be done.

It was the Hebrew month of Kislev in the year 167 B.C.E. (Before the Common Era) and their land of Judea, once independent, had come under the control of the Greek king Antiochus IV, whose empire stretched from Turkey to the ends of Persia. It was at his express order that the troops had entered the Jerusalem Temple and defiled it.

As the village elder, Mattathias was among the first to hear the details. The report was brought by a frantic messenger who had managed to escape Jerusalem and make his way to Modi'in to warn its people of their perilous situation. What he related was worse than anything they could have imagined: Antiochus's soldiers had done more than render the holy Temple impure. They had converted it into a pagan shrine with an image of the Greek god Zeus above the sacred altar.

It was a dark day in Jewish history. Constructed by King Solomon in the 10th century B.C.E., the Temple had stood for some four hundred years until its destruction in 587 B.C.E. by King Nebuchadnezzar, who carried off the Jews to slavery in Babylon. But it had been rebuilt fifty years later, when the Babylonian empire fell and the Jewish exiles returned to Jerusalem.

The Temple symbolized the soul of the Jewish nation, and it was precisely for that reason that Antiochus had desecrated it. The Jews of Judea had always been allowed to observe the rites and customs of their religion. Now Antiochus wanted to wipe it out entirely.

What he wanted the Jews to embrace instead was Hellenism, the Greek way of life. All the other conquered people in his empire had done that. For them, though, it was easier: they already worshiped pagan gods, and adding a few Greek gods and enjoying Greek pagan festivities wasn't much of a change. To the Jews, however, such a thing was unthinkable. They clung to their belief in only one God and to the teachings and laws of the Torah.

They paid a terrible price. Antiochus forbade observance of the Sabbath and festivals, the dietary laws, circumcision, the reciting of Jewish prayers. The penalty for disobedience was death. Jews were killed for studying the Torah. Their sacred scrolls were torn to shred and set on fire. Jews at worship were burned alive when their secret prayer chambers were discovered. Others were struck down for refusing to disregard the Sabbath and for rejecting pagan worship. Now, in the midst of these horrors, came the desecration of the Temple.

In the village of Modi'in, Mattathias wondered out loud why he had been born to see his fellow Jews killed and their beautiful Temple profaned. His five sons listened but said nothing. Furious, they were grappling with their own thoughts. They could not know, nor could their father, that it would be he, Mattathias, who would soon perform an action that would turn the tide – and change the course of history.

Quotations from Josephus, I and II Maccabees, Athenaeus

1. 'The king...built a pagan altar on top of the Temple altar, on which he sacrificed pigs, and the sacrifice he performed was neither lawful nor traditional to the religion of the Jews.'
   — Josephus, Antiquities XII.253 (Loeb ed. Vol. VII, p.128)

2. 'The holy area was filled with excessive revelry. Gentiles lolled about with prostitutes; men had encounters with women within the sacred precincts; and unlawful things were brought inside.'
   — II Maccabees VI.4

3. 'And on the fifteenth day of Kislev, in the hundred and forty-fifth year[1], they built a devastating abomination[2] on the Temple altar, and they built pagan altars all around the cities of Judah.'
   — I Maccabees I.54

4. 'Heliodorus says that Antiochus Epiphanes, the man whom Polybius called Epimanes because of his behavior, mixed the fountain in Antiocheia with wine.'
   — Athenaeus 45c

5. 'And King Antiochus issued a decree to his whole kingdom saying that all should be one people, and that each man should abandon his own customs. And all the peoples obeyed this injunction of the king.'
   — I Maccabees I.41

6. 'And Mattathias saw the blasphemies that had taken place in Judah and Jerusalem and said, alas, why was I born to see this oppression of my people and of the holy city? How can I dwell there when she has been given into the hands of enemies, and the holy place is in the hands of strangers?
   — I Maccabees II. 6-7

[1.] The year that the Syrian Greeks desecrated the Temple was 167 B.C.E. in our calendar.

[2.] Translation of a Hebrew phrase, *shiqqutz m'shomem*

Second Light: The Martyrs

King Antiochus had become impatient. His Hellenization program had gone well throughout his empire, but had made no progress in Judea. Defiling the Temple had been designed to force the Jews into submission. It had apparently only made them more stubborn. The killings went on, but conversions were few.

The king had a new idea. Prominent Jews would be brought before him and told to renounce Judaism and embrace the Greek way of life. He would try argument first. If that failed he would resort to the conventional method.

A group of distinguished Jews were rounded up. Among them was a aged philosopher named Eleazar, a man highly respected for his wisdom and his gentleness by Jew and Gentile alike. Indeed, a few of the king's men knew and admired him. But they showed no sign of recognition as they watched him being dragged before the king.

Antiochus regarded the old man with amusement. "Well now, graybeard," he began, "let me give you some advice before I start with the torture: eat this pig's flesh here and save yourself. I respect you, but how can an intelligent man like you still cling to the religion of the Jews? Why do you refuse to eat excellent meat of an animal that nature has so freely bestowed upon us?"

Eating pig was the last thing in the world that Eleazar would think of doing. He knew he faced a cruel death, but his reply to the king's taunt was calm. Under no circumstances, he said, would he disobey Jewish law.

The king made a simple motion with his hand, and the guards seized Eleazar, stripped him, tied his arms, and whipped him. He was commanded again to obey the king. Eleazar shook his head, and the whipping continued.

At this point, the king's men who knew Eleazar were permitted to see whether they could persuade him. Genuinely concerned for his welfare, they told him that even just pretending to eat the pig was good enough.

Eleazar, unbroken in spirit, was outraged. How could he lend himself to such a lie? It would be shameful. Far better to set an example to the young Jews of how to die happily and nobly in defense of the holy laws. And that is what he did.

It had been an entertaining spectacle for the king, but frustrating, too. Eleazar, he reasoned, was an old man with little left of life. He could afford to be brave. This time the king would choose younger men. Seven brothers were brought before him. He told them to renounce Judaism. He had his guards bring out the instruments of torture. "Be afraid," he said.

The eldest brother replied for them all, saying they were ready to die rather than disobey the commandments. If an old man like Eleazar had died for the sake of their religion, surely they should be willing to as well.

One after the other, the brothers were put to death. By now Antiochus was furious. After them, he had their mother, Hannah, killed as well.

Not everyone behaved like Eleazar or the seven brothers. Some chose physical survival. But many resolved not to disobey the Torah. They were fighting, they believed, for the survival of their nation.

They were right. Stories of Jews who had chosen to die rather than deny their faith began to reach communities throughout Judea, stiffening the resolve of others to hold out against Hellenization. They had a particular impact on Mattathias and his sons in Modi'in. How, they wondered, could they persuade the other villagers to do more than simply suffer the persecution? How could they convince them to fight instead- and fight with more than words? It was time to rise up. It was time for a revolt.

Quotations from II and IV Maccabees

1. 'So King Antiochus sat with his counselors in a high place, with his soldiers at arms around him in a circle, and he commanded his guards to draw aside the Hebrews one by one and make them eat pork and other meat that had been sacrificed to idols. If some of them should refuse to eat the defiled meat, they would be pulled apart on the wheel. Now, when many had been seized and compelled in this way, one Hebrew named Eleazar, of high status and of the priestly class, lawful in his mind, advanced in years, and well-known to many among the king's servants because of his advanced age, was brought before the king.'
   – IV Maccabees V.1-4

2. [Antiochus to Eleazar] 'Old man, before I begin questioning you under torture, I would like to recommend the following: save yourself by tasting of the pork. I respect your age and gray hairs; so why is it that, wise and gray so long, you do not seem to be truly wise and philosophical, but persist in the Jewish religion? Why do you express disgust at the eating of meat, meat which is most excellent and pleasing by nature? It is foolish indeed to deny oneself the enjoyment of pleasures which are without reproach, and to reject the gracefulness of nature because of what you call injustice.'
   – IV Maccabees V.6-8

3. [Eleazar's response] 'We, Antiochus, live our lives as citizens obedient to divine law. We believe that no necessity, no matter how forceful, is greater than our obedience to that law…Thus, to eat defiled things is no small error, since we consider lawbreaking to be equally significant whether in great or small matters. You mock our philosophy, implying that we live as we do without proper consideration. But the law teaches us adequate self-control…. Go ahead, prepare your wheels, make the fire hotter. I will not pity my own old age, not if it means breaking my fathers' law. O Law, my educator, I will not betray you, nor, O Self-control, will I seek to escape you…. My fathers will receive me holy, not fearing mortal necessities. But you are unholy in being a tyrant. You will not, for that, tyrannize over

my inner conceptions of lawful holiness whether be speech or by deed."
– IV Maccabees V.16-38

4. [Antiochus to the Maccabees] 'Youths, it is with a fine feeling that I notice the beauty of each and every one of you. I also greatly respect such a large quantity of brothers. I can only urge you not to yield to the same madness as the old man just tortured. Indeed, I beg you to yield and enjoy my friendship. For I am able to reward those who obey me, just as I punish those who disobey me. Trust in me, then, acquire leading powers even in my affairs, and reject the lawful and traditional constitution of your fathers. Once you have switched over to a Greek way of life, you will acquire new habits and enjoy the pleasures of youth.... Have pity on yourselves, even as I, your enemy, pity you because of your youth and beauty. Will you not take full account of this, that nothing awaits your disobedience but to die on the rack?'
– IV Maccabees VIII.4-10

5. [Maccabees response to Antiochus] "Why do you delay, O king? We are ready to die rather than transgress our fathers' commands. We are rightly ashamed to think of our ancestors, if we do not show obedience and a shared sense of their law. King, partner of unlawfulness, do not pity us when you really hate us. Your pity is more hateful to us than death, since it offers us an unlawful rescue. You threaten us with torture, having apparently learned nothing from the example of Eleazar. If the older Hebrews have already died enduring your torture, ought the youth not also to die, scorning painful necessity as our educator has done? Do as you please, then, King. Should you take our lives because of our religion, don't think you have truly hurt us. We know we carry away the prize of excellence through our suffering and patience. You, however, because of this despotic murder, in divine justice will endure the eternal torture of fire."
– IV Maccabees IX.1-9

6. 'But the mother [known in later tradition as Hannah] was especially worthy of wonder and commemoration: even when she saw all seven of her sons dying in a single day, she bore it well because of her hopes in the Lord. Filled with noble mind,

and casting off womanly thinking in her manful anger, she encouraged each of them in the language of their fathers, saying to them, "I do not know how you came into my womb. I did not give you the breath of life. I did not arrange your bodies' limbs. Therefore, I hold that the founder of the world and creator of mankind and of all things will have pity and give back the breath and life to each of you, since you have neglected your own selves on account of his laws."'
– *II Maccabees VII.20-23*

7. [just after Antiochus has asked the mother to intervene and persuade one of her sons to yield] 'But leaning over close to him, she mocked the cruel king, speaking thus, in the paternal tongue: "My son, pity me. I carried you in my womb for nine months, nursed you three years, and brought you up to your present age, bearing the full burden of your education. I ask you, my child, to look up at heaven and look at the earth, and, seeing all they contain, recognize that God made it all, including the human race, out of things that were not. Do not fear this executioner, but show yourself the equal of your brothers. Accept death, so that I may receive you back with pity among your brothers."'
– *II Maccabees VII.27-9*

Third Light: The Revolt

The center of the village of Modi'in was filled with people, standing sullen and anxious under the watchful glare of soldiers. The entire community had been rounded up and was now ranged in front of a rough pagan altar, topped by an image of the Greek god Zeus. To one side of the altar, there was a tethered pig. At the head of the front row stood Mattathias and his five sons.

The ceremony was about to begin...

The soldiers were there because King Antiochus was angry. The Jews were refusing to give up their faith for his. He had struck at Jerusalem, the heart of Judea. He had taken over their Temple, forbidden the practice of Judaism, and filled the city with the trappings of Greek paganism. He had overthrown their leaders, including the high priest, and appointed his own men in their place.

As more and more Jews fled Jerusalem, Antiochus resorted to more forceful measures, ordering his troops to patrol all the other Judean villages. That was why they were now in Modi'in.

The ceremony began with a brief address by the soldiers' commander. He had come to Modi'in, he said, to instruct the villagers in the noble worship of the god Zeus. An animal would be sacrificed on the altar, and they, the Jews, would show their acceptance of the new faith by tasting the flesh of the offering. That was what the king had ordered, and the king's will would be done, he said, tapping the hilt of his sword.

No one stirred, but all eyes turned to Mattathias, the village elder. He stood motionless, staring ahead, giving no sign of his thoughts.

The commander knew that if Mattathias could be won over, the entire village would follow. He called on him to be the first to come forward and carry out the order of the king. He promised him and his sons money and honor. He asked Mattathias to take a position at the altar.

Only then did the white-haired Mattathias turn to face the officer. Speaking loudly, so that all his people could hear, he told him that he and the others would not obey. He locked eyes with the officer in challenge. The villagers waited. What would Mattathias do? And what would they themselves do? And how would the king's officer react?

Suddenly there was movement, slow movement, and the spell was broken. One of the Jews had stepped forward into the center clearing and was walking past the guards toward the altar. There, to everyone's surprise, he announced that he was willing to make a sacrifice. The sight of the knife being handed to him enraged Mattathias. In a fury he rushed forward and slaughtered the traitor. Then he killed the officer and pulled down the pagan altar. Before the astonished troops could take in what had happened, the sons of Mattathias and the rest of the villagers rushed them and killed them, too.

History doesn't record how a unit, however small, of well-trained, well-armed soldiers could be overpowered by unarmed villagers. But they had encountered no active resistance before and had expected none at Modi'in. They were therefore not as alert as they might have been and were taken completely by surprise.

It was all over in minutes. The villagers marveled at their success. They were alive! They had not betrayed their faith! And the representatives of the tyrant lay dead.

There was no time to celebrate. The army would be sending in a large retaliatory force as soon as they learned what had occurred. The villagers would have to abandon Modi'in without delay. But they would not merely seek a place to hide. They would find somewhere they could prepare for a real battle. They had struck at the enemy that day. Now they would continue to do so. The revolt was on.

Quotations from I Maccabees

1. "And the assistants to the king spoke to Mattathias, saying, 'You, who are a great and respected leader in this city, and supported by sons and brothers, come forward first and perform the command of the king, just as the gentiles have done, and the men of Judah, and the ones left behind in Jerusalem. You and your family will then be among the friends of the king, you will be honored with silver and gold and with many rewards."
   — *I Maccabees II.17-18*

2. "And Mattathias replied to them, speaking in a loud voice, 'All the gentiles dwelling in the household that is the kingdom of the king may obey him, leaving behind the religion of their fathers, and joining in what he commands. Still, my sons and my brothers and I myself will continue in the way of our fathers. God forbid we should abandon the law and its justice. Nor shall we be persuaded by the speeches of the king to transgress our own religion, whether to left or to right."
   — *I Maccabees II.19-22*

3. "And Mattathias saw and was filled with zeal, and his insides trembled, and he was very angry at the crime, and he ran at the man and slew him on the altar."
   — *I Maccabees II.24*

4. "Everyone who feels a zeal for the law and wants to keep the covenant, let him come out and follow me."
   — *I Maccabees II.27*

Fourth Light: The Resistance Fighters

In the space of a few terrible minutes, the normal world of the pious, hardworking farmers of Modi'in had come crashing down. They would be abandoning their lands, with little hope of return. Ahead of them lay the life of outlaws.

There was no time to lose. The move would be made at night, using the shield of darkness to evade the Greek patrols. They would take to the hills, which they knew well and where they would have good protection and good visibility.

By the appointed departure time, all were gathered in the center of Modi'in, carrying the supplies that they could not load onto carts and animals. Led by Mattathias, his sons, and other young leaders of the community, they set out into the gathering dusk.

How was it that they were not quickly wiped out by Greek reinforcements sent to replace the soldiers they had killed? Probably the authorities thought the Jews would take refuge in another village or in the nearby caves. Even when they found out about the hiding place in the hills, they surely thought the rebels would have to emerge sooner or later in search of food and water. In any case, it was not worth the trouble to mount a considerable force to comb the forested hills for so insignificant a quarry. They had no reason to imagine that a pitiful bunch of fugitives from an obscure Judean village would pose a threat to their rule. They were wrong.

For a year they left the rebels alone. The rebels used the time well, training themselves and rousing the spirit of resistance among the other villagers of Judea. Young volunteers soon began to join the rebels, and they, too, were given a crash course in the art of guerrilla warfare.

Mattathias's middle son, Judah, was looked to as the new warriors' leader. For inspiration and tactics, Judah had the example of David, who killed the far mightier Goliath. The Greeks had many more arms and men, but a small group with light weapons, like David's, could move quickly. The Greek troops were unfamiliar

Hanukkah in Eight Nights

with the terrain; the Jews were natives. The soldiers could expect no support from the hostile population; to the Jews, the local inhabitants were their brothers and sisters. Above all, the troops were mercenaries, fighting for their living; the Jews would be fighting for their lives.

Here and there, the Jews attacked, ambushing small patrols of Greek soldiers and carrying off their weapons. If they observed the approach of a strong enemy contingent, they simply melted into the countryside. In the first year, the rebels limited themselves to the surrounding area. They did not venture into the walled city of Jerusalem, the headquarters of the Greek army and administration. They were not yet prepared to penetrate a fortress that formidable. But that would come sooner than anyone expected.

At the end of that year Mattathias died, and his sons took his body from the hills at night and buried him in his village of Modi'in. He had been an inspiring leader and the guiding spirit of the resistance movement. And he had created something much greater than he or anyone else knew.

Quotations from I Maccabees

1. "And he fled, he and his sons, into the mountains, and they left behind all they had in the town."
   – *I Maccabees II.28*

2. "And the people of Israel mourned Mattathias with a great lament."
   – *I Maccabees II.70*

Bronze Prutah of John Hyrcanus I (135-104 B.C.E.)

Obverse: Hebrew inscription in wreath:
   "Yehohanan the High Priest and the Council of the Jews"

Reverse: double cornucopiae with pomegranate between horns

Fifth Light: Judah the Maccabee

On his deathbed, Mattathias had named his son Judah his successor in commanding the rebels. Judah was a popular man, pious like his father and an equally formidable leader. He was known by all as "the Maccabee," which is the Hebrew word for "hammer." But there is a similar-sounding word meaning "extinguisher," and some scholars have wondered if Judah was called Maccabee because "he extinguished Hellenism in Judea." Whichever is correct, it accurately describes Judah, who hammered his foes and extinguished their plans to destroy the Jewish way of life.

The rebel group Judah commanded was a larger and more experienced force than it had been a year earlier. But although the men skirmished here and there with the enemy's patrols, they had not yet met Antiochus's army full on. Judah recognized that he needed many more men and that they had to be spread out all through the different districts of Judea, ready at any moment not only to operate in their own area but to help out wherever else they were required. They would be on day-and night-call by a local commander, and when they were done they would return to their ordinary lives. Innocent farmers, they would be "invisible" to the king's troops. And because they had their own homes and raised their own animals and grew their own crops, they would relieve general headquarters of the problems of food, shelter, and the movement of supplies.

The system would also provide more eyes and ears for the Maccabees, as Judah's followers – the resistance forces – now called themselves. For example, working in their fields, they might spot a unit of the enemy's army heading north. The news would be transmitted – by a runner or by flag signal – to the next village, and from there to the next until it reached the district commander, who would relay it to Judah's headquarters. Other farmers in villages along the enemy's route would file similar messages. From the collection of such reports, general headquarters might discern a pattern to the enemy's movements and plan an ambush.

Information on the enemy's overall intentions was far more difficult to come by. For that, Judah relied on undercover agents, or spies, who operated at great risk right in the heart of Jerusalem.

Sure enough, it soon became difficult for Antiochus's army to patrol freely in Judea. The countryside was largely under the control of the Maccabees, with Greek rule in the province virtually confined to Jerusalem alone. Antiochus's commander in Judea realized that he had a full-scale rebellion on his hands and that to crush it he needed far more troops. But explaining the reason to his superiors was embarrassing. How could he report that his troops were being beaten by a ragtag, poorly armed bunch of farmers? Still, the report had to be sent, even though it meant his certain dismissal from the imperial army.

The result was to affect far more than the future of one high-ranking Greek officer. Judah and his Maccabees were about to face their most critical test since Modi'in.

Quotation from I Maccabees

1. "Then Judah, the one called Maccabee, replaced his father in command. His brothers came to his assistance, as did all those who had adhered to his father. All of Israel was glad to fight the war.... Judah donned his breast-plate like a giant, adding his warrior's armor, and proceeded to fight wars, protecting the camp with his sword. His deeds were those of a lion; and he was like a young lion who roared for the hunt. He sought out and prosecuted wrongdoers and had the popular troublemakers burned at the stake.... The doers of evil were greatly troubled, while safety was made to prosper under him."

— *I Maccabees III.1-7*

Sixth Light: The Test

In the royal palace at Antioch, capital of Antiochus's empire, the king was in a fury. He had decided to launch a huge military campaign in the eastern territories of Parthia, Persia, and Media, which were threatening to secede, and he was in the midst of preparations when news reached him of the trouble in Judea. He was outraged, for he had been led to believe that all was under control in the Jewish province.

Summoning his general staff, he ordered that an appropriate force of battle-hardened troops be sent immediately to crush the uprising. The task was entrusted to General Apollonius, the governor and military commander of Samaria, who was all too eager to show an unruly province that he was in control.

But Judah, commander of the rebel Maccabees, had spies, and they told him about Apollonius's plan. Two thousand soldiers, they said, would be marching south from Samaria to Jerusalem. They would be passing close to the region where Judah was hiding, although whether or not they would attack or make straight for Jerusalem was uncertain.

That was enough for Judah. He decided to attack the enemy while it was on the mach, when the troops were most vulnerable – moving in tightly packed formation, less alert than they would be on the battlefield, and not ready for action.

Apollonius's troops marched southwards in a compact column, each man almost bumping into the man in front. They followed the military pattern conceived by their hero, Alexander the Great, but Apollonius had decided he didn't need protection of flanking cavalry armed with swords and lances or of scouts to warn of upcomoing dangers. After all, he was only fighting a bunch of untrained, underarmed rebels. The sight alone of his two thousand man force would intimidate them.

A few miles northeast of Judah's hiding place, the Samaria-Jerusalem highway entered a narrow gully, a passage that wound uphill for about a mile. The enemy columns approached it, unaware that the Maccabees awaited them. One group was posted in concealed positions along the eastern edge of the passage, another along its western edge, and a third at its southern exit. A fourth unit assembled a short distance from the northern entrance, ready to close the trap as soon as the entire enemy force was within.

The first of Apollonius's soldiers came marching into the passage. The men in ambush waited silently. When the lead group was almost through and about to reach the southern exit, Judah gave the signal to attack.

The Maccabees at the southern end sprang from their positions, rushed through the narrow exit, and fell upon the surprised enemy vanguard with slings, daggers, sickles and swords captured in earlier skirmishes. The troops in the lead were killed before they even had a chance to use their weapons, and those immediately behind them were driven back. But the main body of soldiers, ignorant of what was happening ahead, kept pressing forward, squeezing their already crowded comrades into an immovable mass. And they kept coming, each file bumping into the stopped file in front. The entire first formation of one thousand men was soon brought to a bewildered standstill, pressed in front by Judah's sealing unit, in the back by their own rear soldiers, and on either side by the banks of the gully.

That was the moment for the ambushers on the top of the banks to let fly with their slings against the long column of wedged-in troops. They followed with close-quarters action, rushing on the enemy with an array of short, light, and lethal weapons. The soldiers were helpless, weighed down by their heavy arms and equipment, with no room to maneuver into the combat position, and unable to hurl their long spears.

Apollonius, hearing the cries of battle and concerned at the halting of his lead formation, spurred his horse and tried unsuccessfully to press forward to learn the reason. For a few moments he towered above the writhing mass of battling soldiery in the gully. And then he toppled down, killed by one of the Maccabees. As new of his death swept rapidly through the enemy ranks, adding to their disarray, Judah's fourth unit reached the northern end of the passage and attacked the formation in the rear. The battle was over. The Maccabees had won.

In the village of Judea, the people celebrated. Judah and his combat commanders were more restrained. They knew that Antiochus would not rest, and his next attack would be more formidable. They had to devise new concepts and new methods of warfare to met a new challenge.

It was not long in coming.

Quotation from I Maccabees

1. "And Apollonius gathered the peoples, a great force from Samaria, in order to fight Israel. And when Judah became aware of this he went out to meet him, and defeated him, and killed him. Many were wounded and killed, and the survivors fled. He took their equipment, and personally claimed Apollonius' sword, which he proceeded to fight with from then on."
   – *I Maccabees III.10-12*

Double prutah – see page 71

Seventh Light: The Battles

Judah knew that another attack was inevitable, and another and yet another, until final victory, and that each would be more powerful than the last. He would need to keep coming up with new ideas, for the Maccabees would always be outnumbered and outarmed. For the moment, he concentrated on familiarizing his men with the new weapons they had captured – the swords, the more sophisticated slings, the javelins, the spears, the bows – while he devised unconventional ways of using them. Although the odds against him were great, Judah had two advantages: the spirit of his people and knowledge of the terrain on which they would be fighting. The hill country of Judea was his home ground. No one knew better than he how to exploit it to military advantage.

In the Greek capital, Antiochus listened with mounting rage to the report of Apollonius's defeat and ordered a new force, twice the size of Apollonius's, to be sent into Judea as quickly as possible under General Seron, a trusted commander. Seron chose an easier and safer, though longer, route along the Mediterranean coastal plain. He would proceed southward almost to Jaffa, then turn inland to climb the Judean hills to Jerusalem. From Jerusalem, he would move out into the countryside, wipe out the rebels, and reestablish Greek authority in the villages.

There was one big flaw in Seron's choice of route. The moment he turned inland and marched openly through the plains to reach the Judean foothills, Judah required no spies to know what he would do next, for the only track from there to the heights ran up a steep ascent to the pass of Beth Horon. Judah thus had ample time to prepare. He placed his men behind the protective boulders and shrubs near the top of the pass and along both sides of the passage leading up to it. The Maccabees numbered one thousand, Seron's troops four thousand.

The soldiers made the hard climb up the long, winding, uneven slope and had almost reached the top when Judah gave a signal and the unit at the head of the pass went into action. Archers and slingmen, using weapons captured from Apollonius, killed the enemy's lead men and sent the oncoming files staggering back on their comrades. Others of Judah's men, wielding captured swords,

Hanukkah in Eight Nights

rushed on the teetering foe, thrusting those behind back down the slope. Judah then signaled the units positioned along the enemy's sides, and they too opened an attack. The enemy formations broke up, and the troops ran helter-skelter down the hills, with the Maccabees in hot pursuit. General Seron had been killed early in the battle, and now his leaderless troops offered no resistance to the Jewish rebels.

King Antiochus retaliated with a force of twenty thousand soldiers under two generals, Nicanor and Gorgias. So certain was Nicanor of a quick victory that he asked several slave dealers to come along, too, and invited them to put in their orders for Jewish slaves even before the battle began. Before venturing into the hills, the Greeks set up their base camp at Emmaus, in the lowlands, some fifteen miles northwest of Jerusalem. Judah's force had now grown to six thousand, split into four formations under himself and his brothers Johanan, Simon, and Jonathan. By a series of deceptive actions, they lured Gorgias and a large number of his men out of Emmaus and into the hills, then made a surprise dawn raid on Nicanor's units in their camp and sent the survivors scattering. When Gorgias looked down on the plain and saw the camp in flames, he and his men, too, took flight.

It took Antiochus another year to raise an army large enough to face the Maccabees again. But it, too, fell to the rebels. Its commander, realizing that he had overrated the fighting spirit of his own men and underrated the Jews, returned to the capital of Antioch in defeat, abandoning huge stocks of weapons and equipment to the Maccabees. He would return to Judea, he swore, with a much larger force that ever before.

Yes, thought Judah, there would certainly be a repeat performance, but he estimated it would take the Greeks a long time to prepare. He knew what to do in the meantime, now that the Maccabees were stronger than they had ever been and were in full control of rural Judea. He would proceed with the aim that he, his father, and his brothers had set themselves when they had sat in Modi'in three years earlier, mourning the defiling of the Jews' sacred shrine. They would go up to Jerusalem to cleanse the Temple and rededicate it. That would be their real victory.

Quotations from I Maccabees

1. "And Seron, the leader of the Syrian forces, heard that Judah had gathered a force and assembly of the faithful, ready to go out with him to war. And he said, 'I will make a name for myself and be famous in the kingdom by fighting Judah and those with him, the ones who regard the word of the king as nothing.' So he made ready to march, and a mighty army of the wicked marched with him for his aid, to punish the sons of Israel."
   — I Maccabees III.13-15

2. "Lysias chose Ptolemaios the son of Dorumenes and Nicanor and Gorgias, men who were in high standing with the king, and he sent with them forty thousand foot soldiers and six thousand cavalry to attack the land of Judah and destroy it, as the king had commanded. And they set out with all their force and they arrived, making their entry near Emmaus in the foothills."
   — I Maccabees III.38-40

3. "And Judah and his brothers saw the evils were at their fullest, and the forces were pouring over their borders. And they thought of the king's speeches in which he had vowed to drive the people to its final destruction. And each man said to his neighbor, 'let us effect the purification of our people: let us fight on their behalf, and on behalf of the holy things.'"
   — I Maccabees III.42-3

4. "Now Jerusalem was an uninhabitable wilderness, none of her children came and went. The sacred shrine was trampled upon, and sons of foreigners were in the Akra citadel [opposite the Temple Mount]; it became a lodging place for the gentiles. Joy was removed from Jacob. Flute and harp left off playing."
   — I Maccabees III.45

5. [Judah and his troops have come to Maspha opposite Jerusalem] "They fasted that day and put sack-cloth and ash over their heads and tore their clothes. And they laid open the book of the law, which the gentiles had sought to illustrate with images of their idols."
   — I Maccabees III.47-8

Eighth Light: The Temple Regained

Judah and his Maccabees were encamped on the outskirts of Jerusalem. They had encountered no opposition en route, and there was none now. The city was still, with no troops in sight, not even guards to prevent them from climbing the ruined walls that the enemy had battered in an earlier rampage. The Greek soldiers had decided to do their fighting from a fortress know as the Acra. They had good reason to want its protection: if the Jews had defeated Antiochus's mighty army, what chance would they have in open battle? And so they took refuge in the Acra as soon as they learned that the Maccabees were on their way to Jerusalem.

Meeting no opposition, Judah and his men made straight for the Temple. There would be time later to tackle the fortress. But as they approached, they were assailed by arrows showered from the parapets and recesses of the Acra. Judah's own archers, armed with captured bows, now went into action, while his lead men proceeded to the Temple. The sight that greeted them was one of utter desolation.

They found the Temple laid waste, its altar profaned, the gates destroyed, the courts overgrown, the buildings in ruins. As distressed as they were, they didn't take the time to grieve – which was all they had been able to do three years earlier in Modi'in. Instead they began immediately to cleanse the sacred shrine of all traces of idolatry and to restore it to the service of the Lord. While some of the fighting men kept the enemy from leaving the Acra, others set about clearing the Temple area, purifying the sanctuary and removing the stones that defiled it, repairing the buildings and courts, and restoring the interior.

Then came the great day. On the twenty-fifth of the month of Kislev, the Temple was reconsecrated by the Maccabees and their followers in the most moving ceremony of their lives. It was indeed one of the most moving occasions in all of Jewish history.

The retrieval of their holiest shrine from the hands of the pagan was seen by the faithful of Judea as a miracle, the divine reward for their unwavering resolve and their active fight against impossible odds to preserve their traditional beliefs and customs. The few triumphed over the many, and their victory and the dedication of the Temple were celebrated by the community for eight days.

That was the beginning of the festival of Hanukkah, which has been observed every year since 164 B.C.E. by Jews throughout the world. "Hanukkah" is the Hebrew work for "dedication," which was what the festival was called at the time. Later, it was also called the Festival of Lights, because of the tradition we most associate with Hanukkah – the lighting of the Hanukkah menorah, or "hanukkiah" in Hebrew.

Why do we light the Hanukkah menorah and why do it for eight days? What does it have to do with the Maccabees? According to one story, when Judah and his men entered the Temple, they found that all the pure oil needed for the Temple lamp had been defiled, except for one small container that still bore the High Priest's seal showing it had not been touched. But this one container held only enough oil for a single day. Miraculously, however, it kept the Temple menorah burning for eight.

Another story told how the Maccabees found eight iron bars in the Temple – possibly Greek spears – and stood them up and lit lights on them.

Whatever the origin of the Hanukkah traditions we observe today, they help us remember what the Maccabees did for the Jewish people, how they spurred them to cling to their beliefs even under the most cruel persecution, to fight tenaciously for the preservation of their Jewish identity and to make Judea an independent Jewish state. Without them, who knows who we would be. The Maccabees' determination to safeguard their faith and liberty sustained the Jewish people throughout the long, dark centuries of exile, and led to the rebirth of the State of Israel.

Quotations from I Maccabees

1. "They woke early, the twenty-fifth day of the ninth month (that is Kislev) of the 148th year.[1] They held a festival according to the law on the new sacred altar for whole burnt offerings they had made. At the very same time of year and day in which the gentiles had polluted the altar, it was renewed with songs and citherns and harps and cymbals. The whole people fell on their faces and bowed and praised to heaven the One who had set them on the right path again."
   — I Maccabees IV.52-5

2. "Judah and his brothers and the whole assembly of Israel established that these days of the year should be celebrated as being the days of the renewal of the sacred altar, at the appropriate time, year after year, for a total of eight days, starting from the twenty-fifth of Kislev, with pleasure and good cheer."
   — I Maccabees IV.59

[1.] *The year that Judah and his men cleansed and rededicated the Temple was 164 B.C.E. in our calendar.*

Hanukkah Chronology
and Questions for Discussion

Hanukkah Chronology

323 B.C.E. Death of Alexander the Great
Kingdom is split into three parts for the three Greek generals: Antiochus rules Greece, Ptolemy rules Egypt, and Seleucus rules Syria and much of Asia Minor.

200 B.C.E. Syrian Greek King Antiochus III conquers Palestine.

190 B.C.E. Battle of Magnesia; Romans cross into Asia for the first time and defeat Antiochus III.

175-164 B.C.E. Reign of Syrian King Antiochus IV "Epiphanes." He appoints hellenizing High Priests: Jason from 175 to 172 B.C.E. and then Menelaus, from172 to 162 B.C.E.

168 B.C.E. Antiochus IV Epiphanes attacks Egypt and plunders the Temple.

167 B.C.E. Mattathias and his sons revolt against the king's officers. The Temple is desecrated by the Syrian Greeks.

166 B.C.E. Mattathias dies, Judah the Maccabee becomes leader of the revolt.

165 B.C.E. The Maccabeans battle the Greek general Lysias.

164 B.C.E. March Antiochus IV Epiphanes issues an amnesty decree allowing the Jews to return to their own homes "to use their own food and to observe their own laws as of yore."

164 B.C.E. December Judah's men clean the Temple, make a new altar and furnish it. They celebrate the rededication for eight days.

162 B.C.E. Antiochus V Eupator (son of Atiochus IV Epiphanes) relinquishes his father's attempt to convert the Jews to Hellenism and writes his general Lysias that "the Jews of the realm should live undisturbed and attend to their own concerns," agreeing "to give them back their Temple and to permit them to live after the manner of their ancestors." Appointment of a High Priest from the Jakim family who calls himself Alcimus. Judah refuses to recognize him, touching off more internecine unrest.

161 B.C.E. Nicanor, who had fought with some of the Hellenized Jews, is killed in battle with Judah, who re-takes Jerusalem and celebrates his victory as a festival. Judah sends a delegation to Rome, and they return with a treaty between Rome and "the nation of the Jews." The Greek King Demetrius I's general Bacchides, accompanied by Alcimus and a professional army, defeats Judah, and Judah dies in battle. His brother Jonathan becomes leader of the Maccabees.

156 B.C.E. Jonathan makes peace with the Syrian Greeks.

152 B.C.E. Jonathan accepts the office of High Priest from Alexander Balas, although he is not from a priestly family. He becomes a Seleucid official.

146 B.C.E. The Romans destroy Carthage.

143 B.C.E. Jonathan is taken captive and murdered by a Syrian Greek battling for power. His brother Simon takes over the leadership and expands the borders of Jewish control.

140 B.C.E. Simon becomes high priest "until a faithful prophet shall arise" and wins freedom from the Selucids. He is thus the first leader of the Hasmonean Dynasty, a Jewish state within the Seleucid Greek empire.

139 B.C.E. The Senate recognizes the Hasmonean dynasty when a delegation from Simon visits Rome.

134 B.C.E. Simon is assassinated by his son-in-law, and is succeeded by his third son, John Hyrcanus. Antiochus VII reconquers Jerusalem but grants it autonomy. John Hyrcanus is succeeded in 103 B.C.E. by his son, Judah Aristobulus (Aristobulus 1), the first Hasmonean to adopt the title of king.

103 B.C.E. Alexander Jannai, becomes king. During his reign, which lasts until 76 B.C.E., the state expands its borders. However, the rivalry between him and the Pharisees drags the Jews into a civil war, which ultimately costs them their independence.

76 B.C.E. Queen Salome Alexandra succeeds her husband Jannai. She appoints a Pharasaic leader who favors rabbinic leadership. The rabbis decree that all boys are to be taught to read the sacred texts, instituting widespread literacy.

63 B.C.E. Pompey conquers Jerusalem. Under the Romans, Hyrcanus II (Salome's son) serves as High Priest under Antipater the Idumean, followed by Antigonus, who is executed in Antioch, ending Hasmonean rule.

37 B.C.E. Herod, the son of Antipater, who had married the Hasmonean princess Mariamne, granddaughter of Hyrcanus II, becomes King. Herod rules from 37 B.C.E. to 4 B.C.E.

Questions for Discussion

1. Who was fighting whom in the Maccabean wars?

2. What were the Maccabeans fighting for?

3. Did the Maccabees fight on the Sabbath, and why? Discuss the rabbis' adage that "The Sabbath is given to man and not man to the Sabbath."

4. What was the Hasmonean dynasty, and how long did it last?

5. What has the ring of truth about the story of the Maccabean war, and what might be "apocryphal"?

6. What empire was in decline during this period, and what empire was getting stronger? What options did the Jewish leadership have?

7. When Judah established Hanukkah as a holiday of eight days, what other Jewish holiday already existed with an eight day celebration?

8. How did contact or interaction with Hellenism affect the development of Judaism?

Stories from 1 Maccabees
Adapted from the King James Version translation (1611)

The books of the Maccabees have been preserved in the Apocrypha, the ancient Jewish books in Greek which are not part of the Tanakh, or Hebrew Bible. Here are some of the stories from I Maccabees, beginning with the division of Alexander the Great's kingdom, and ending with the rise of the Hasmonean Dynasty under Simon.

Alexander, son of Philip the Macedonian, defeated Darius, king of the Persians and the Medes, and became king. Alexander fought many battles, conquered strongholds, and ruled over countries, nations, and princes for twelve years. He fell sick, and summoned his most honored generals, to divide his kingdom among them.

Alexander died, and his generals took over as rulers, each in his own place (Ptolemy in Egypt, Antiochus in Greece and Seleucus in Syria). They all put crowns on, and so did their sons after them, and instigated many evils on the earth.

Antiochus Epiphanes was the son of Antiochus the king, and he began to rule the Greeks. He gave some men in Israel permission to build a gymnasium in Jerusalem, according to the customs of the non-Jews.

Antiochus made war against **Ptolemy** king of Egypt, captured strong cities in Egypt and plundered them. Then he went up against Israel and Jerusalem with a great multitude.

He proudly entered the sanctuary and took the golden altar, the menorah, costly vessels and utensils, the table for the bread, the curtain, the Torah crowns, the hidden treasures and the gold decoration on the front of the Temple.

There was great mourning in Israel in every place.

Hanukkah in Eight Nights

Two years later the king sent his chief collector of tribute to Judah with a large army. He spoke peacefully but in deceit and then suddenly fell upon the city, plundered it, burned it, tore down walls and houses, seized cattle and took women and children captive. Then Antiochus fortified the city of David with strong walls and towers and stored arms and food there. The residents of Jerusalem fled; the city became a dwelling of strangers and wicked men, and her sanctuary became desolate as a desert.

King Antiochus wrote to his whole kingdom that all should become one people by adopting Greek customs. His letters told the Judeans to profane the Sabbaths and festivals, to pollute the sanctuary, to build altars for idols, to sacrifice unclean animals and to leave their sons uncircumcised.

The king wrote: "Whosoever does not do what the king commands shall die." He commanded the cities of Judah to offer sacrifice, city by city.

Many people forsook the law and did his bidding, committing evils; others went into hiding.

Mattathias, a priest, went down from Jerusalem to Modi'in. He had five sons: **Yochanan**, **Simon**, **Judah**, **Eleazar** and **Jonathan**. He lamented the sacrileges being committed, and he and his sons mourned greatly.

The king's officers came to Modi'in to enforce the Greek sacrifices, offering Mattathias and his sons gifts (in the year that corresponded to 167 B.C.E.). Mattathias told them,

"My sons and my brothers and I will live by the covenant of our fathers. We will not obey the king's words by turning from our religion either to the right hand or to the left."

A Jew stepped up in the sight of all to make a sacrifice upon the altar in Modi'in, according to the king's order. When Mattathias saw this, he was inflamed, and he ran and killed the man upon the altar, crying out,

"Whoever is zealous for the law and upholds the covenant, come with me!"

Mattathias and his sons fled to the hills and left all that they had in the city, and many followed them.

Antiochus's army attacked them on the Sabbath, and they refused to engage in battle on that day, losing many people in the battle. After that, Mattathias and his recruits decided to fight back if they were attacked on the Sabbath. They found new recruits and went around the countryside to pull down altars and recover the law.

Mattathias grew weak and died in the year that corresponded to 166 B.C.E. He was buried in the tomb of his fathers in Modi'in and his son Judah took command of the fighters.

Judah was like a lion in his deeds, like a lion's cub roaring for prey.

He went through the cities of Judah; he destroyed the ungodly out of the land.

The Greek general **Apollonius** gathered together Gentiles and a large army from Samaria to fight against Israel. When Judah learned of it, he came forth to meet him, and he smote and killed him. Many fell, wounded, but the rest fled. Judah took the sword of Apollonius, and fought with it for the rest of his life.

Seron, the commander of the Syrian army, went out to battle against Judah in the hills of Beth-horon.

When Judah's men saw the army coming to meet them, they said to Judah, "How will we be able, so few of us, fight against so great and strong a multitude? And we are ready to faint, for we have eaten nothing all day."

Judah answered, "They come against us with a lot of pride and iniquity to destroy us and our wives and our children, and to take plunder from us; but we fight for our lives and our laws."

Judah rushed suddenly against Seron and his army, and pursued them down the hills of Beth-horon to the plain. Eight hundred of them were slain, and the rest fled into the land of the Philistines.

King Antiochus heard these reports, and was full of anger. He gathered a very strong army, opened up his treasury, gave his soldiers a year's pay, and ordered them to be ready when he needed them. Yet, the tributes he could collect in the region were diminished by dissension and plague. In order to go to Persia to collect additional tributes there, King Antiochus put **Lysias** in charge of his son Antiochus and the region from the river Euphrates to the borders of Egypt. He gave Lysias half of his troops and elephants so that he could send a force against Israel and the remnant of Jerusalem.

Lysias sent his generals, **Nicanor** and **Gorgias**, forty thousand infantry and seven thousand horsemen to make war against Judea, and they encamped near Emmaus.

Slave traders went to the camp with immense amounts of gold and silver, expecting to buy Israelite slaves from the Greeks after the battle.

Jerusalem was uninhabited, a wilderness; none of her children went in or out; the sanctuary was trampled, strangers were in the fort, the joy was gone and the flute and the harp ceased to play.

Judah appointed captains for the people, in charge of thousands and hundreds and fifties and tens. He told those who were building houses, or were newly wed, or were planting vineyards, or were fearful, to return home, as the law allows.

Then Judah's army marched out and encamped south of Emmaus.

In the battle that ensued, they crushed the Greek army even though the Greeks had more men and were better armed.

Lysias heard about the defeat of his army, and the next year he sent even more men to subdue Judah's army, but the Jews defeated the Greeks again.

Then Judah and his brothers said, "Behold, our enemies are crushed; let us go up to cleanse and dedicate the sanctuary."

They went up to Mount Zion. The sanctuary was desolate, the altar profaned, and the gates burned. Shrubs grew in the court and the priests' chambers had been destroyed. Judah's men cleansed the sanctuary and removed the defiled stones. They took uncut stones and built a new altar, made new holy vessels, and brought the menorah, the altar, and the table into the Temple. They set loaves of bread on the table and hung up the curtains.

Early in the morning on the twenty-fifth day of the month of Kislev, in the one hundred and forty-eighth year (corresponding to December 25, 164 B.C.E.), they dedicated the Temple with songs and harps and lutes and cymbals.

They celebrated the dedication of the altar for eight days, and offered a sacrifice of deliverance and praise. There was very great gladness among the people.

Judah and his brothers and all the assembly of Israel determined that every year at that season the days of dedication of the altar should be observed with gaiety and gladness for eight days, beginning with the twenty-fifth day of the month of Kislev, and they fortified Mount Zion.

Judah and his brothers Simon and Jonathan and their men fought many battles with many tribes, Greek and non-Greek, and made peace with others. They tore down altars with pagan gods, and returned victorious. Antiochus heard about it and he was astounded. He became sick, and appointed his friend **Philip** as regent for his son, who was also named Antiochus, and then the elder Antiochus died, and his son became king.

The new king **Antiochus Eupator** tried to re-take Judea in the year corresponding to 163 B.C.E. His forces under Lysias, his general, were joined by mercenary forces from other kingdoms and from islands of the sea. He had 100,000 foot soldiers and 20,000 horsemen, and thirty-two elephants trained for war. The soldiers showed the elephants the juice of grapes and mulberries, to incite them to fight. They distributed the elephants among their warriors, who had coats of mail and brass helmets. Each elephant had a harness which supported a covered wooden tower, and inside each tower rode an Indian driver and four armed men.

When the sun shone upon the shields of gold and brass, the hills glistened and shined like burning torches.

Judah and his army advanced to the battle, and six hundred men of Antiochus's army fell.

Eleazar, one of the Maccabee brothers, saw that one of the beasts was equipped with a royal harness, and was taller than the others, and he thought that Antiochus was on that elephant. Running into the battle, he stabbed the elephant from beneath, and killed it, but it fell to the ground on him and killed him, too. Then Judah's men saw the strength of Antiochus's army and ran away.

Antiochus's army went up to Jerusalem, camped near the Temple, and set up siege towers and instruments to throw fire and stones, to shoot arrows and to throw catapults. The Jews also made engines against their engines, and the two sides fought for many days. The Greeks had consumed the local stored food. It was a sabbatical year, food was scarce and the vessels were empty. Lysias wanted to get back to the seat of his government because Philip, Antiochus's regent, was trying to seize control there. So the Greeks sent the Jews an offer of peace, that they would be allowed to live by their laws as they did before. Then the Greeks returned to Antioch, where they fought Philip and regained control of the city by force.

Other Greek generals continued to fight the Jews, including Nicanor. His army was finally defeated after men came out of villages from all around Judea, out-flanked the enemy's soldiers, and drove them back.

Demetrius, the son of **Seleucus**, came from Rome with an army and defeated Antiochus and Lysias, killing them. He colluded with ungodly people among the Jews, including **Alcimus**, who wanted to be High Priest. They went to Judea under the command of **Bacchides**.

The **Hasidim** spoke in peaceful terms to them, and deceitfully pledged not to harm them, but then killed sixty men in one day. Judah's forces fought back, whereupon Alcimus appealed to the Demetrius, who sent Nicanor, one of his honored princes, and a man that hated Israel, with instructions to destroy the people. Nicanor's army was finally defeated after Judah's men came out of the villages from all around. They outflanked the enemy's soldiers, drove them back and killed Nicanor and all the soldiers. Then the land of Judah could rest for a while.

Judah heard of the fame of the Romans, who were mighty but friendly towards people who entered into alliances with them. He heard of the Romans' wars in Gaul, where they conquered the local people and levied taxes on them, and how they went to Spain and took possession of the silver and gold mines there. He heard how they gained control of distant lands with thorough planning, and even defeated Antiochus, great king of Asia, and took his best provinces, including India, Media and Lydia.

Judah also heard that the Romans were loyal to their friends and those who relied on them, and that not one of them put on a crown or was clothed in purple to make themselves important. The Romans had made a senate house, and every day three hundred and twenty senators sat in that council in order to govern the people well. They entrusted the government to one man each year to rule the country.

So Judah sent emissaries to Rome to establish an alliance and to free Israel of the yoke of the Greek empire. They went to Rome, a very long journey, and they came to the senate and said,

"Judah the Maccabee and his brothers, and the people of the Jews have sent us to you to establish an alliance and a peace with you, to be your allies and friends."

The Romans were pleased, and wrote a letter to the Jewish people on bronze tablets, which they sent to Jerusalem. In the letter, they said

"Good success be to the Romans and to the people of the Jews at sea and on land forever, and may sword and enemy be far from them."

The Roman letter said that they agreed to act as allies, to refrain from giving grain, arms, money or ships to any enemies, and to abide by their obligations as allies without deceit, and that the people of the Jews had the same obligation. The letter also said the Romans had written to Demetrius, asking why the yoke was so heavy on the Jews, adding, "If they complain any more against you, we will do justice by them, and fight with you at sea and on land."

But the battles with the Greeks continued, and Judah's armies had to keep fighting Bacchides and Alcimus. Judah died in battle, and his brothers **Jonathan** and Simon buried him in the tomb of his fathers in Modi'in. Jonathan became the leader of the Jews in place of Judah. The Greeks fortified cities in Judea, put aside stores of food, and there was two years of rest in the land before Jonathan had to fight them again. Alcimus started to demolish an inner courtyard in the sanctuary, but he became ill, and died. Simon fought Bacchides, who finally made an agreement with Jonathan to free Jewish captives, and went back to his own land. Jonathan began to govern the people, and destroyed the ungodly men in Israel.

Alexander Epiphanes, the son of Antiochus, landed in Ptolemais and he reigned there. King Demetrius assembled his troops and also sent letters to Jonathan petitioning for peace and allowing him to recruit troops. Jonathan came to Jerusalem to read the letters to the people. Hostages from the tower were delivered to Jonathan, who delivered them to their parents. Jonathan began to rebuild Jerusalem and repair the city. Only in Beth-zur did some remain who had forsaken the law and the commandments, for it served as a place of refuge.

King Alexander sent Jonathan a letter appointing him High Priest, and sent him a purple robe and a gold crown. Jonathan put on the robe, recruited troops, and gave them armor.

Then King Demetrius sent Jonathan a letter, releasing him from tributes, salt taxes, royal levies, and agricultural tithes for Judea, Samaria and the Galilee, and offering freedom for festival days. He offered to employ Jews in his own forces, to allow the Jews to govern themselves and to live by their own laws. He offered Ptolemais as a gift for the sanctuary, to endow its expenses.

But Jonathan and the people did not believe King Demetrius, remembering the evil that he had done in Israel. They were pleased with Alexander, who was the first to seek an alliance, and they remained allied with him.

The armies of the two Greek kings fought each other, and Alexander's men defeated Demetrius's army; Demetrius was killed. Later, Ptolemy gave Alexander his daughter **Cleopatra** in marriage, and they celebrated the wedding at Ptolemais with great glory. Jonathan went to Ptolemais to meet Alexander and Ptolemy, and gave them presents of silver and gold.

Some lawless men from Israel came with accusations against Jonathan, but the king would not hear them. The king honored Jonathan and clothed him in purple, and made him governor of his province. Jonathan returned to Jerusalem with peace and gladness.

But Demetrius's son **Demetrius** had a general, Apollonius, who continued to fight the Jews. Jonathan and Simon defeated Apollonius, and King Alexander honored Jonathan and sent him a gold buckle, and gave him Ekron and the area around it.

King Ptolemy of Egypt had gathered many troops, like the sand upon the seashore, and he had designs against Alexander's kingdom. He set out for Syria, and peaceably gained control of the coastal cities, leaving garrisons there. Jonathan went to meet the king at Jaffa, and they greeted each other, and stayed there overnight. Ptolemy thus gained control of the coastal cities as far as Seleucia.

King Ptolemy sent envoys to Demetrius, offering an alliance, saying, "I will give you in marriage my daughter who was Alexander's wife, and you shall reign over your father's kingdom. I regret that I gave him my daughter, because he has tried to kill me." Ptolemy wanted Alexander's kingdom, so he took his daughter away from Alexander and gave her to Demetrius. Then Ptolemy entered Antioch and put two crowns upon his head, the crown of Egypt and the crown of Asia. Ptolemy proceeded to march against Alexander. Alexander fled into Arabia for protection, but **Zabdiel** the Arabian took off Alexander's head and sent it to Ptolemy. Three days later, King Ptolemy died, and his troops in the strongholds were killed. By this means, Demetrius became king.

Jonathan went with his men to Jerusalem to take the tower there. Ungodly Jews went to King Demetrius to tell him what Jonathan was doing, so the king wrote to Jonathan to tell him not to lay siege to the tower, but to come to Ptolemais in haste. Jonathan went to Ptolemais with gifts of silver, gold, clothing and other presents, and was well received by the king. The king confirmed Jonathan as High Priest, and Judea and Samaria as free of tribute, and Jonathan promised to pay the king three hundred talents.

When Demetrius saw that the land was quiet and there was no resistance against him, he sent his forces home, which made the troops who had been his father's forces hate him. Seeing this, **Tryphon**, who had been with Alexander, went to Simalcue, an Arab who was bringing up Alexander's son Antiochus, and asked him to give him Antiochus to rule in place of his father, Alexander.

Meanwhile, Jonathan asked Demetrius to remove his troops in the fortress and strongholds in Jerusalem who were fighting Israel. Demetrius agreed, and asked Jonathan to send troops to help him. Jonathan sent three thousand men to him in Antioch, who fought until the people in the city asked for peace. The Jews were honored in the sight of the king and returned to Jerusalem.

King Demetrius had peace, but estranged himself from Jonathan. Tryphon returned with the young Antiochus, who was crowned. The soldiers Demetrius had sent home fought Demetrius, and Tryphon captured the elephants and conquered Antioch. Then the young Antiochus wrote Jonathan, confirming him in the priesthood and as ruler of the four districts. He sent him golden vessels and granted him the right to drink from gold cups, to wear purple and to wear a golden buckle. He made Simon captain from Tyre to the borders of Egypt.

There were more battles in the land, and in the plain of Hazor Jonathan and his men were ambushed, and fled, then turned back, and routed the enemy. Then Jonathan returned to Jerusalem.

Jonathan renewed the peace with the Romans, and exchanged letters, and wrote to the Spartans as well. But the battles with the Greeks continued. Jonathan perished in battle against Tryphon, and Simon took his bones and buried them in Modi'in, the city of his fathers. Simon built a monument of polished stone over the tomb of his father and his brothers.

Tryphon killed the young king Antiochus and put the crown on his own head. Simon fortified strongholds in Judea, with towers, walls and gates, and stored food. Then he sent King Demetrius a letter with gifts, asking for peace and relief from Tryphon, who continued to plunder. Demetrius replied, confirming the agreements he had made. **Simon** became the high priest, commander and leader in the year 170 (corresponding to 142 B.C.E.), which the Jews called the first year of Simon the High Priest.

Finally, after the Maccabees had besieged Gaza, conquered it, and cleaned it of idols, the people in the tower in Jerusalem, who were dying of hunger, sued for peace. Simon made peace, and cleaned the tower of its pollutions. Simon and his company entered the tower with thanksgiving and palm branches, and with harps and cymbals and stringed instruments, and with hymns and songs, because a great enemy had been destroyed and was gone from Israel.

Simon's son **John** had reached the age of manhood, and Simon appointed him commander of the army. The land was at peace for the rest of Simon's life. He sought the good of his nation, was honorable in his acts, and took Jaffa for a harbor, where he made an entrance to the islands of the sea.

Simon strengthened all those of his people that were brought low, searched out the law, and took away wicked people. He beautified the sanctuary and made more vessels for the Temple. When they heard in Rome, and as far away as Sparta, that Jonathan was dead, they were very sorry, but they wrote Simon to renew the friendship and alliance they had made with Judah and Jonathan and the brothers.

The people thanked Simon and his brothers for repulsing Israel's enemies and establishing its freedom. They made a memorial in bronze recording Simon's feats that was set upon pillars on Mount Zion, and copies were laid up in the treasury.

The Jews tilled their land in peace, and the trees bore fruit. Old men sat in the streets and talked together of good things, and the young men put on warlike and glorious apparel. Simon supplied the cities with food, and munitions, established peace in the land, and Israel rejoiced with great joy. Each man sat under his vine and his fig tree, and there was none to make them afraid.

– Adapted from I Maccabees by Marian Scheuer Sofaer

Notes on the ancient sources

I Maccabees was probably written originally in Hebrew, but survives only in its Greek translation. It covers the forty-one year period following the accession of Seleucid emperor Antiochus IV Epiphanes in 175 B.C.E. and gives an account of the Maccabeean struggle. Scholars believe it was written in the second half of the 2nd century B.C.E. by a Jew in Israel who either lived through the events or heard about them from eyewitnesses.

II Maccabees was written originally in Greek towards the end of the 2nd century B.C.E. It is an abridgement of a work by Jason of Cyrene, a contemporary of Judah, and it covers the fifteen year period from 176 B.C.E. to shortly before the death of Judah in 160 B.C.E.

Other ancient sources for the Maccabeean war and its period are a philosophical book known as IV Maccabees, which is from the end of the 2nd century or beginning of the 1st century B.C.E., the Book of Daniel, which scholars believe was written in Judea during the reign of Antiochus, several books of the Jewish historian Josephus (*The Antiquities of the Jews*, Books 12 and 13 and *The Wars of the Jews*, Book 1), written in the 1st century B.C.E., as well as books by two Roman historians, *The Histories*, Books 22-39, by Polybius (*The Histories*, Books 22-39) from the 2nd century B.C.E., and Livy's *History of Rome*, written in the 1st century B.C.E.

– Moshe Pearlman

Traditional Hanukkah Recipes

Latkes (Potato Pancakes)

2 pounds potatoes (peeled)

½ cup flour

1 small, minced onion

1 or 2 eggs, or 1 egg and 1 egg white

1 oz. melted butter or
   a quarter to a half cup of oil

Salt and pepper to taste

Oil for frying

1. After the potatoes are peeled, use a grater with large holes to grate the potatoes, or use a machine to mince them.
2. Squeeze out the excess water.
3. Mix flour, eggs, salt and pepper into the grated or minced potatoes. This is your batter.
4. Heat a thin layer of oil to a high heat in a skillet, preferably a non-stick one. Drop in a large spoonful of the batter. Fry until the potato pancake is golden, then flip and fry the other side.

Makes 10-12 small latkes

Sufganiyot (Jelly Doughnuts)

For the dough:
2½ teaspoons active dry yeast or 5 tablespoons of fresh yeast
4 tablespoons granulated sugar
1½ cup lukewarm water
4 tablespoons oil
pinch of salt
4 cups all-purpose flour
4 egg yolks
zest of one lemon or orange
1 teaspoon vanilla extract
1 tablespoon cognac

Other ingredients:
jelly or jam for the filling
confectioners sugar for sprinkling
oil for deep frying

To make the dough, dissolve the yeast and 1 tablespoon of the sugar in ½ cup lukewarm water. Set aside for about 5 minutes until foamy.

Sift 4 cups of flour into a large bowl. Add the yeast, warm water, eggs yolks and rest of the ingredients. Stir to make a dough. Knead for 10 minutes on a lightly floured board, incorporating more flour as necessary, until the dough is soft, silky, and pliable. Form into a ball. Place in a bowl and turn to coat the dough all over. Cover with plastic wrap and leave to rise until twice its original size. This will take about 2 hours. When well risen, punch down the dough.

Roll the dough to 1 inch thick and cut out rounds with a cup. Brush the top with a little oil to avoid dryness, and allow to rise for another 10-15 minutes.

Heat the oil to a high heat (about 375°). Fry doughnuts in the hot oil, 4 or 5 at a time, until puffed up and golden brown, and place on a paper towel. Fill with jelly or jam by piping it in with a pastry bag with a small opening or injector. Dust the filled doughnuts with confectioners sugar.

Hlawa – An Iraqi Hanukkah Treat

1 cup unbleached flour

3 tablespoons vegetable oil

2 cups sugar

1 cup water

2 tablespoons rose water

Syrup:

Mix water and sugar in a bowl and set aside.

Dough:

In a non-stick saucepan heat oil and sauté flour until it becomes very light brown.

Lower heat and very slowly add ¼ of the syrup mixture, stirring constantly with a wooden spoon. When it almost dries out add another ¼ of the syrup. Continue stirring and adding syrup until the dough looks like caramel.

Add the rose water and stir for a few minutes.

Put it in a square glass dish to cool off. Eat it in pita bread.

– Aaron Matityahu

**Silver tetradrachm of Antiochus IV (175-164 B.C.E.)
minted in Acco**

Obverse: Head of Antiochus IV
Reverse: Zeus seated on throne holding Nike and scepter

A Very Brief Jewish History
from the Patriarchal Period to the Maccabees

1900 - 1500 B.C.E.: Age of Patriarchs (Middle Bronze Age).

The stories of the patriarchs in Genesis tell us that Abraham journeyed from Ur of the Chaldees in Mesopotamia to Canaan, and that the twelve tribes of Israel descended from his family. The compelling stories of the patriarchs and their families are the glue for the common origins of the Jewish people.

Scholars have searched for archaeological remains to illuminate the history of the period. Pottery and the remains of structures from the patriarchal period in Canaan are plentiful, but there have been few finds with writing, and no historical record documents Abraham's journey or the lives of the succeeding generations. However, The Ebla cuneiform tablets, written in the third millennium B.C.E., and found at Tel Mardikh in Syria, mention a place called Ur, possibly the same place as in the Genesis story.

Egyptian records refer to battles with the semitic Hyksos. The story of the expulsion of the Hyksos from Egypt after they had been in power there for 100 years is the closest historical parallel to the story of the exodus of the Hebrews from Egypt. However, the expulsion of the Hyksos was in 1570 B.C.E., and the Exodus story would be about 1200 B.C.E.

1500 - 1250 B.C.E.: Egypt to Canaan

When the Egyptians reasserted dominance over Egypt, they expelled as many foreigners as they could. Archaeologists have questioned whether the Hebrews migrated from Egypt to Canaan or whether they adopted the exodus story as their own while they were living in Canaan. The evidence is confusing. The Egyptian word "Habiru" means "fugitive" or "refugee," and that may be related to the word "Hebrew," whose root can mean to pass, or cross over (in the sense of travel). The Merneptah victory stele, from the reign of the son of Ramses II (who has been considered the Pharaoh of the Exodus) around 1220 B.C.E., mentions Israel as a people: "Israel is laid waste, its seed is not." It lists defeated and expelled peoples, one of which is described as "now living in Canaan."

Whatever their origins, it is clear from archaeological remains in villages in Israel dating to 1200 B.C.E. that the Hebrews there had a distinct identity. A lack of pig bones in their settlements suggests that these early Israelites did not eat pork.

1200 to 920 B.C.E.: Canaan.
Establishment of the Kingdom.

After the collapse of the city state system in the late Bronze Age, the Hebrew tribes settled in the hill country and managed to make a living there. They learned to build lime-plastered systems to reserve water for the dry periods. They worked the land by creating systematic terracing, which was laborious, but gave them enough acreage to raise cereals. They cultivated almonds, figs, grapes and other fruits on the hillsides.

Archaeologists have found practically no evidence of cities being destroyed in this period. Some scholars argue that the conquest of Canaan described in Joshua and Judges may have been an internal population migration into the hills. Around this time, the Philistines, a sea people coming from the Aegean region, established five cities near the coast of the Mediterranean. There was friction between the Hebrews in the hill country and the coastal, urban Philistine population.

The Hebrews in the northern part of Canaan had more arable land than those in the southern areas, and they were more prosperous, and more engaged in trade. Yet there were cultural common denominators, including their connection to a common patriarchal heritage.

Around 1000 B.C.E., the Hebrews finally dominated the land of Canaan, and united Israel in the north, and Judah in the south, to form a single state under a single monarch, King David, and later his son, Solomon.

920 B.C.E. to 597 B.C.E.: Two Kingdoms.
Fall of the Northern Kingdom.

Following the death of King Solomon, under his son Rehoboam, the kingdom again split in two, with Judah and its capital Jerusalem in the south, and Israel and its capital Tirzah in the north. Within a century of Solomon's death, Judah was reduced to a small state. The northern kingdom, wealthier because of its fertile land, built several fortresses and its new capital at Samaria.

The prophet Amos understood the impending danger of Assyrian conquest. In the mid-eighth century B.C.E., Amos attacked the luxury and indifference of the Northern Kingdom under Jeroboam II, who ruled from 788-747 B.C.E.

The prophet Isaiah was concerned about the rise of Assyrian power, and in 742 B.C.E., he called on the Jews in dramatic language to accept the one God. He urged them to be mindful of the commandments in all of their activities, in order to avoid the wrath of God and the destruction that was soon to follow. Isaiah's plea for moral leadership and his eloquent language still has a universal appeal.

In 722 B.C.E., the Assyrians, under their King, Sargon II, punished a rebellion in Israel by conquering the northern part of the kingdom. The Assyrians exiled nobles, landowners, craftsmen and musicians.

Many Israelites took refuge in Judea in the south, following others who had fled Assyrian repression. Meanwhile, the development of the Hebrew alphabet from its Phoenician origins encouraged the establishment of a scribal school in the court. Jerusalem became a major city whose Yahweh-based religion and veneration for the Aaronite priests absorbed the Moses and El -centered traditions of the north.

King Hezekiah gave the priests more power, and the centrality of their role and the Temple rites is reflected in the Torah. In 701 B.C.E., Hezekiah prepared Jerusalem for an Assyrian siege by diverting the water of the Gihon spring through a tunnel in the bedrock to the city. A celebratory inscription describes the meeting of the stone cutters who started at each end of the tunnel, 581 yards apart, when they met in the middle.

In the following years, during King Josiah's reign, the prophets Zepheniah and Huldah warn that unless the people carry out God's commandments, the Babylonians will destroy them. Jeremiah's prophecies also predicted the disaster of the Babylonian conquest, but hoped for consolation upon an eventual return from exile.

586 to 538 B.C.E.: Fall of Southern Kingdom, Exile.

The Babylonian King Nebuchadnezzar exiled many of the leading Jews from Jerusalem in 597 B.C.E. Eleven years later, in 586 B.C.E., under the reign of Zedekiah, Nebuchadnezzar destroyed both the Temple and the city. Following standard practice, the most prominent citizens of Judah- professionals, priests, craftsmen, and the wealthy aristocracy, around 10,000 in all- were forced to relocate to Babylon.

Ezekiel, a young priest, who was exiled with his countrymen, composed his prophecy in response to the exile. The Judean peasantry was allowed to stay behind, and continued to maintain contact with their deported brethren.

The fall of Judah splintered the Jewish community into three parts, the community in exile in Babylon, the original community in Judah, and a refugee community in Egypt. The Jews in Babylon were in close proximity with each other, and able to form a community where they could retain their religion, practices, and philosophies. Descendants of this important community continued to prosper in what is now Iraq for the next two thousand years.

In Babylon, after the exile, the prophet known as Second Isaiah focused on a vision of the One God which was full of hope, superseding the stern rebukes of earlier prophets. This God would forgive Israel and lead the people back to Jerusalem.

538 to 332 B.C.E.: The Return under the Persians.

The Persian King Cyrus conquered the Middle East and put an end to the Babylonian empire. Cyrus's Zoroastrian beliefs led him to prepare for the final struggle between good and evil. To achieve this, he sent many people whose gods he thought could be beneficial back to their native lands to worship there. The Jews were allowed to return to Jerusalem to rebuild their Temple.

Ezra made the reading and study of the Torah a focal point of the life of the reconstituted Jewish population in Jerusalem. However, in spite of Ezra's exhortations to return, many Jews stayed in Babylon, where they had built a strong community. They established the distinguished academies in Nehardea, Pumbedita and Sura, which dominated Jewish scholarship for several centuries.

For another two hundred years, Persia dominated much of the Middle East and Egypt. Israel was a tribute state of Persia, and the High Priests in the Temple replaced the kings as the leaders of the people.

The new Temple was dedicated in 515 B.C.E. Fifty years later, the Persian governor Nehemia rebuilt the walls of Jerusalem and enacted reforms allowing the collection of tithes and observance of the sabbath.

The text of the Torah had become canonized by about 450 B.C.E., and from that time it was preserved to the letter. When the Dead Sea Scrolls, which are over two thousand years old, were found, they showed that a Torah made by a scribe living in the first century B.C.E. was almost identical to the text of the Torah as we know it now.

332 - 63 B.C.E.: Greek Dominance.

Alexander the Great conquered Persia in 332 B.C.E., and Israel fell under Greek dominance. Greek philosophical ideas spread throughout the empire.

After Alexander's death, the Greek empire was divided among his three top generals. Seleucus inherited the Middle East and Mesopotamia, starting a line of Seleucid Kings who ruled Israel., Ptolemy ruled Egypt, and Antiochus ruled Greece.

The Greeks introduce the notion of naturalized citizenship. For the first time, Jews, already dispersed throughout the Greek empire, become citizens of other states, while retaining the religious and cultural integrity of their communities.

In 168 B.C.E., Seleucid king Antiochus IV tried to eradicate Jewish practices. He persecuted the Jews who refused to assimilate to Greek culture, desecrated the Temple, and touched off a Jewish revolt under the Maccabees.

After the Maccabees' victory against the Syrian Greeks, the Jews had a succession of Hasmonean kings for about 150 years. Starting in 169 B.C.E., these generations had an interesting, if bloody, history.

Alexander Jannai, who reigned from 103 B.C.E. until 76 B.C.E., expanded the borders of the Jewish state. He favored the Sadducees, and his tyrannical treatment of the Pharisees pushed them into a civil war, which weakened the state.

In 76 B.C.E., Queen Salome Alexandra, who as a woman could not become High Priest, appointed her son to that position. However, she increased the importance of rabbinic leadership by appointing her brother, the leader of the Pharisees, to lead the Sanhedrin, which functioned as the Council of State. The rabbis decreed that all boys must be taught to read the Torah, and instituted a system of required elementary education. From this point on, Jewish boys were expected to be versed in scripture and able to read and write.

Descendants of the Hasmoneans continued to rule from 63 B.C.E. until the Roman conquest in 70 AD. This period of self-rule produced an important literature and new practices, which enabled the Jews to sustain their traditions and culture when they were exiled once again.

63 B.C.E. - : Roman Dominance. Diaspora.

In 63 BC, Judah (or Judea in the Latinized version) became a protectorate of Rome. The ruling Roman authorities endeavored to regulate trade and to maximize tax revenue. Religious and economic tensions flared up. The Essenes and other sects maintained severe practices, and the Pharisees and the Saducees were at odds with each other over questions of orthodoxy and interpretation of religious law.

In response to the tragic Judaean revolt of 70 C.E., the Romans destroyed Jerusalem, struck coins celebrating "Judea capta," and carted the Temple treasures, the Temple menorah, and Jewish slaves off to Rome. They annexed Judea as a Roman province, and systematically drove the Jews from their native land, completing the dispersion of the Jewish people that had started under Assyrian and Babylonian conquerers.

After the destruction, a small community of scholars survived in Yavneh, determined to preserve Jewish learning. From then on, the leaders of the Jewish community were not priests who inherited their status, but scribes and teachers who earned the title of rabbi.

Josephus, the Greek-speaking Jewish historian who participated in the revolt against the Romans, but eventually tried to persuade his fellow Jews to desist in the rebellion, wrote a history of the Jews that covers the Maccabean wars and the revolt against the Romans. I and II Maccabees also tell the story in gruesome detail, and references to these wars and the revolt against Rome also survive in the works of the Roman historians Livy and Polybius.

The Babylonian Talmud, written over the next several centuries, kept the intellectual spark of the Jewish soul alive, and provided a literature for communal debate that had a bonding effect on a dispersed people. It was written partly in Hebrew and partly in Aramaic, which had been the dominant Jewish language for everyday life for centuries. Aramaic receded in importance as a spoken language after the Roman conquest as the expelled Jews started to adopt the languages of their host countries, but some important prayers in the liturgy, such as the mourners' prayer, are still recited in Aramaic.

Throughout their history, the Jews found in the Torah a framework to understand the world, a history of the universe and of the Jewish people, a code of moral conduct, and the foundation for a legal system. The Torah became, in effect a civilization in a book. Because it was portable, it fostered the centralization of ideas, achieving a shift from "atoms to bits," from land to knowledge.

Sustaining a civilization in diaspora requires that the "bits" that form its backbone never be lost. To this end, Jewish law contains exquisitely precise, and sometimes arcane, prescriptions for copying, preserving, and studying the Torah. The Maccabees were fierce defenders of the law, and required strict adherence to its practices. Their success in maintaining loyalty to the sacred texts, and the continuing centrality of those texts in Jewish life had a unique result: the Jewish people have achieved and sustained the elusive goal of 100% literacy – at least among men – for the last 2,100 years.

– Alain Rossmann and Joanna Hoffman

Bronze double prutah of John Hyrcanus I (135-104 B.C.E.)

Obverse: two cornucopiae tied with ribbon. Inscription:
"Yehohanan the High Priest, Head of the Council of Jews"

Reverse: Crested helmet with cheek pieces

 **Coins of the Maccabees**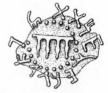

Gifts of "gelt" or money have been part of the Hanukkah celebration since Talmudic times. What was the actual money that was used during the days of the Maccabees?

The first coins ever struck by a Jewish ruler for use by Jews in the ancient land of Israel were struck by High Priest John Hyrcanus I (135 B.C.E.-104 B.C.E.). Hyrcanus, whose Hebrew name was *Yehohanan* was the son of Simon the Maccabee and nephew of the great hero Judah Maccabee. Hyrcanus was succeeded for a brief period by his brother Aristobulus (104-103 B.C.E.), whose Hebrew name, *Judah*, was used on his coins. Both Hyrcanus and Aristobulus proclaimed on their coins that they were issued by the "High Priest and the Community of the Jews." The son of Hyrcanus I was Alexander Jannaeus, also known as Yannai (103-76 B.C.E.), who proclaimed himself not only High Priest, but also "King" on his coins. His Hebrew name was Yehonatan. It seems probable that another group of Maccabean coins with the name "Yonatan" were struck during the reign of Jannaeus's wife and successor Salome Alexandra, in the name of her son Hyrcanus II, who was High Priest, but not king. Mattathias Antigonus (40-37 B.C.E.), a nephew of Hyrcanus II, was the last of the Hasmonean leaders and he also issued the last coins of the Maccabean dynasty. In order to compete with his rival for the crown, Herod I (the Great), Antigonus also issued some larger bronze coins of 8 and 4 prutot in size.

Mattathias Antigonus also issued the most famous ancient Jewish coin, which depicted the Temple's Menorah on one side and the Showbread table on the other. It was forbidden to reproduce sacred objects from the Jerusalem Temple, but Antigonus did it anyway, in order to try to rally the Jewish people behind him as the last reigning member of the Maccabean dynasty.

The coins of the Maccabees were all struck from bronze and were quite small denominations, called *prutot* (singular: *prutah*), about the size of a United States dime. Plenty of larger silver and bronze coins circulated in ancient Israel during the time of the Maccabees, but these were coins of the Seleucid Kings of Syria, the Ptolemaic Kings of Egypt, and other Greek rulers. It was, however, up to the local rulers to fulfill the need for small change in the marketplace of the rather poor land of ancient Israel.

The Maccabean rulers strictly adhered to the Biblical admonition against graven images in Exodus 20:4. Thus, unlike the various Greek rulers, we do not have any portraits of the Maccabean kings from their coinage. Instead they used mostly agricultural designs, such as cornucopias, pomegranates, grains, lilies, and palm branches. The anchor, a maritime symbol, is also used on some Maccabean coins, along with the sun surrounded by a "diadem" which is an ornamental headdress signifying sovereignty. One rare Maccabean coin depicts a war helmet and finally, of course there is the rare coin of Mattathias Antigonus with the Menorah and Showbread table.

Holding in your hand a coin of the Maccabees gives you the thrill of connecting to the ancient independent Jewish state that was the forerunner of the State of Israel.

– David Hendin

Dreidel Game

Dreidels are used for a gambling game that appears to date back to the period of Syrian Greek rule in Israel, when it was illegal for Jews to study Torah. The students kept spinning toys close by, ready to be pulled out if Greek soldiers came to check on them. That way they could pretend they were playing, rather than studying Torah.

Stock up on pennies before the holiday.

Give each player an equal number of pennies or tokens. Before the game starts, each player puts a number of pennies in a pile, or kitty (all players contribute equally). Each player by turn spins the dreidel, which is marked with a Hebrew letter on each of its four sides. When the dreidel falls, that player takes from the kitty of coins, or contributes to the kitty according to which letter is face up:

 נ   ג

Nun   **Gimel**
none   *take all*

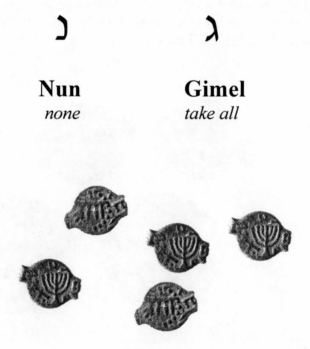

The letters form a sentence in Hebrew: *Nes Gadol Haya Sham.*
A great miracle happened there.

If you buy an Israeli dreidel (*s'vivon* in Hebrew), it will have a Peh
instead of a Shin. That is because the sentence reads: *Nes Gadol
Haya Poh.* A great miracle happened **here**.

The gambling game dates to antiquity, but the meaning ascribed to
each Hebrew letter derives from medieval German usage:

Dreidel comes from the German "drehen," or turn.
The rule for Nun (no action) comes from "nicht," or nothing.
The rule for Gimel (take all) comes from "ganz," or all.
The rule for Hey (take half) comes from "halb," or half.
The rule for Shin (put one in) comes from "stell," or put in.

ה   ש   (פ)

Hey   **Shin**   **(Peh)**
take half   .... *put in one*...........

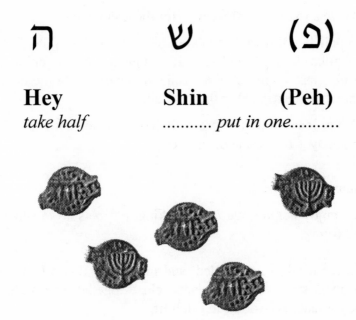

Plan Ahead
for
Home Hanukkah Celebrations

1. Make or buy a hanukkiah (a Hanukkah menorah with 9 candles, one of which is the "shamash" candle used to light the others). A simple hanukkiah can be made out of clay or modeling material or out of a strip of wood or metal; 3/8ths inch stainless steel nuts from the hardware store, glued to the base, are the right size to hold Hanukkah candles.

2. You'll need 44 candles or wicks and oil for all eight nights (2+3+4+5+6+7+8+9). Make sure you have matches.

3. The traditional foods for Hanukkah are latkes (potato pancakes), served with applesauce or sour cream or yogurt, or sufganiyot (jelly doughnuts). Children can make festive sugar cookies with Hanukkah cookie cutters.

4. Have a roll of pennies ready for the dreidel game.

5. Small bundles of chocolate coins covered in gold foil are popular during Hanukkah. If you give money to children as gifts, ask them to give some to charity, a time-honored practice mentioned in the Talmud.

6. Your local Jewish store will have music tapes, ideas for holiday activities, and supplies.

Precautions:

Children enjoy helping with the cooking, but be sure to supervise deep-oil frying.

Don't leave candles unattended, and make sure that a homemade hanukkiah is safe. Candles placed close together can melt, and hanukkiyot made of wood can catch fire.

Printed in the United States
39062LVS00004B/7-114

9 780977 476800